Beyond the Chore Chart:

Chores, Kids, and the Secret of a Happy Mom

by Kimberly Eddy

www.BeyondtheChoreChart.com

Table of Contents

Part One:
The Chores Dilemma

Introduction:
"How did you train your children to be helpers?"

It's a question I've gotten frequently, as my children have gotten older, and have become quite helpful, not just at home, but towards others in the community.

I am not even sure if I want to call them "children" anymore. Every one of my five are now speeding towards adulthood, having entered their teen years. My oldest has graduated from our home school. Next summer, my son will be working at a summer camp, far away from home.

I'm no longer a mom of many little ones.

This question also came up from some discussions on my blog following my shoulder surgery a few years ago. I was gushing about all of the help my children had provided me with, because it was a world of difference from the last time I had surgery or an injury. The difference of *actually having help* in this situation was extremely obvious to me.

A year later, when I needed emergency gall bladder surgery, my children again rose to the challenge and helped out above and beyond the call of duty.

In fact, I wrote some of this book while holed up in my room recovering from that surgery.

"Don't worry mom, we've got this!" they assured me.

While recovering, I didn't have to do a thing. I didn't even have to worry about what *wasn't* getting done. No one died, and the house didn't catch fire. The Christmas décor was put away, meals were made, and one child in particular remembered to remind me to take my prescriptions. They each took turns coming upstairs to see if there was anything I needed.

Was the house spotless? *No.*

Though it wasn't spotless, the house was quite clean, tidy, and running smoothly without me micro-managing it all, which was all that mattered.

This glorious and blessed end result didn't just happen.

I didn't just hang a chore chart on the wall, and somehow, intuitively, they knew what to do to keep the household running smoothly.

Though it wasn't spotless, the children were able to keep the house quite clean, tidy, and running smoothly without me micro-managing it all.

No, this end result came about from two things:

1. God's grace

2. Years of patient and frustrating training

As I've pondered this question: "How did you train your children to be helpful?" I've had to think back, long before the days of my children taking care of the household while mom was laid up in bed. I used some of their help in writing this book, too, as they helped me remember some of the training I did with them to encourage them in this way. I'm thankful for their input into this book you're holding.

I also realized some areas where I failed, and had the opportunity to learn on this road of child rearing. I've gotten lots of on the job training as a mom, that's for sure!

I hope this book is a help and a blessing to you, as you search for ways to train your own little helpers.

Kimberly Eddy
March 2012

1
The Story of Slobalina

My mother used to call me *Slobalina*.

Part of it was because we are two people who are wired completely different. At the time, I thought I was just defective as a person, because no matter how hard I tried, I couldn't seem to make things good enough or clean enough for my mom's high standards of housework. My mom didn't know how to convey how to do something she did quite naturally and automatically, and I couldn't wrap my head around how to do what she was asking me to do.

This is something we need to get out of the way right from the start of this book. I'm not Suzy Homemaker and I'm not Supermom.

My mom and I butted heads most of my growing up years, and some of my adult years over this one issue. I'm a slob and she's not. She sees (and apologizes for) messes that don't exist. For years, I couldn't see messes that she saw and demanded I clean up.

I feel like this is something we need to get out of the way right from the start of this book.

I'm not Suzy Homemaker and I'm not Supermom.

Whew. There. I said it.

My homemaking skills are constantly and continuously improving through hard work and determination on my part, but homemaking and cleaning are not natural gifts of mine by any stretch of the imagination. I have had to put forth significant effort in that area – more effort than I require for most other tasks.

Let me put it this way: you'd probably feel comfortable coming over to my house instead of feeling like an inadequate failure. But you'd also not be grossed out.

As a child and teen, I would spend all weekend cleaning my room, before finally, proudly showing it to mom.

"Ugh, piles there, and there, and what is that over there? *You call this clean?!?*"

I understand now that mom wasn't trying to be harsh. She was frustrated. She couldn't understand why this was so complicated for me, since I could effortlessly do things that were complicated to everyone else (including her).

As I said, we're wired differently.

How could I work all weekend and get results *worse* than what she'd get after an hour in my room?

This pattern continues right into today.

I tell my mom she is never allowed to just stop over. I tell her it's because we're always out doing field trips and cool educational things. She lives about an hour away, so this is practical for both of us.

My mom was frustrated. She couldn't understand why chores were so complicated for me, since I could effortlessly do things that were complicated to everyone else (including her).

The real reason I need a warning is because it takes a week of cleaning to get it clean enough to apologize for what a mess the house is. I'm sure none of you do that with your moms, right?

This issue, for most of my childhood and early in my adult life made me feel quite frustrated. I was a pretty smart person, in all honor's level classes, but I couldn't figure out how to get my room "clean enough" or how to keep it clean. My mom would often express frustration about this specific issue, too.

I started thinking maybe I was just really stupid deep down inside, because I couldn't see the messes she was talking about much less figure out how to fix them.

What's wrong with me?

Natural Born Talents

Now, years later, I see that nothing is necessarily wrong with me. We all have things we're naturally gifted in, and mom is naturally gifted with cleaning and keeping things tidy. I'm naturally gifted in dozens of other things, but not domesticity. Cleaning, for me, takes lots of work and effort, and is very stressful. Cleaning is something I have to really focus in on, and discipline myself to do properly.

As Albert Einstein once said, "Everyone is a genius. But if you judge a fish on its ability to climb a tree, it will live its whole life believing that it is stupid."

Even if we don't have the "housekeeping gene" and even if our children don't have the tidiness gene, we are likely gifted in many other realms. However, just as someone who is not good with numbers still needs to balance their checkbook even if it makes them see stars, we can't ignore housework just because it's not our gift. We still need to clean up after ourselves, of course, but a *different approach* may be necessary.

"Everyone is a genius. But if you judge a fish on its ability to climb a tree, it will live its whole life believing that it is stupid."

~Albert Einstein

You may be wondering why I'm telling you all of this, given that this book is about training our *children* to do chores.

I'm telling you because we need to be careful in how we go about this training. If you're someone who is born organized, with a natural gift for tidiness, you may be very frustrated with a child who is not. And, even worse, you will likely be very frustrating to them.

Even if it comes naturally to you, cleaning does not come naturally to everyone, which is what this book is all about. I want to show you some insight into specific training for chores. I want to encourage you to take the time to show your child exactly how it's done.

When you have five children, as I do, you see that truly every child is wired uniquely. I used to believe that children are a blank slate, and we imprint on them what we want. After having several children, I see most of them were hard-wired even in the womb with their own personality traits and gifts. Watching them grow, and watching their uniqueness all come out as they grow, has been fun to watch.

One of my children is what you would call a neatnik. You could even refer to her as "born organized". If I need something super, ultra tidied up, I call in Esther.

Once, we spent the afternoon at a friend's house for a home schooling moms meeting. The kids were all off playing together. Later, Tammy called me to ask me which of my kids was in so-and-so's room. I was worried as to what was wrong that she was asking, so I asked about the issue outright.

"Oh, nothing's wrong. I just walked past her room only to discover it is cleaner than it was when we moved in. I can see the floor, the drawers are sorted, and there's no mess in the room at all! My daughter told me that your daughter put her to work cleaning."

"Ah, that would be Esther then."

I can assure you, none of my other children would have done that for fun.

Clearly, the neatnik gene is some sort of random mutation that missed me and my other children. The neatness trait also missed my husband.

Just as someone who is not good with numbers still needs to balance their checkbook even if it makes them see stars, we can't ignore housework just because it's not our gift.

How do I know it's something you're born with? Esther started sorting and cleaning as soon as she could walk. I'd come to her crib in the morning, and her blankie would be folded. Not perfectly, mind you, but it would be an incredibly good attempt for a toddler.

Only a minimal amount of intervention is needed to get Esther to do something around the house. I show her how I want it done, and it gets done mostly.

Encouraging or Discouraging?

With other children, to varying degrees, I have to use more intense training, reminders, tricks, prompts, and learning aids to help them not only see the mess but know how to remedy it. If I tell the "neat" child to go clean her room, she walks in and does it. No specifics necessary. If I tell any other child to go clean their room, they would likely stand in the doorway and stare into the abyss for several minutes, trying to figure out what to do first. They may even be trying to discern where the mess even is.

"Mess??!? I don't see any mess! *I wonder what she's talking about...*"

In these cases, as a mom, I need to help show them what to do and how to do it, so as to not frustrate and discourage them.

The repetition of explaining how to clean their rooms, and how to clean up in other parts of the house, starting with me working along side of them, as we'll talk about later, eventually leads to them knowing how to do this on their own with less hand-holding and help. That is the eventual goal (to be able to do it on their own) but it's not always easy to get there. In fact, getting them from point A to point B is what this book is all about!

In speaking of child-rearing, the Bible gives parents this bit of advice, *"Fathers, provoke not your children to anger, lest they be discouraged."* (Colossians 3:21)

"Fathers, provoke not your children to anger, lest they be discouraged." (Colossians 3:21)

The word used in the original text, translated "discouraged" can also mean "disheartened, dismayed, spiritless". That about sums it up, doesn't it?

I don't want to *dishearten* or *dismay* my children. I don't want to crush their spirits in trying to teach them to take care of everyday chores.

Housework is a part of life no matter who you are or what you do. *Everyone* has to learn to clean up after themselves. But, I don't want to leave a bad taste in their mouths for this necessary task. Even the "Slobalinas" of this world will eventually need to keep their own houses clean, even if they hire a maid.

How much easier that task will be if we, as moms, teach them how to complete their chores now in such a way as to help them overcome their lack of natural skill in this area!

Obviously, teaching a child with a natural bend towards tidiness is far easier (though a little convicting) than training up a child like me, who works all day and still has a mess, or who cleans their room only to have it a pig sty in a short amount of time again.

2
The Point of Chores

Let's take a step back for a moment, and talk about the "why" of what we're doing here. What's the whole point of getting your children to help out with chores?

You may think you know why you want to train your children to do chores, but I want to share a few thoughts in this area with you anyway. Humor me.

Training our children to do chores takes far more work and effort than if you were to just do the job yourself in the first place.

Initially, chores may seem like a good way for a busy mom to not be quite so overworked, but as we'll be discussing soon enough, you'll be disappointed, at least at the start. After all, as we'll soon see, training our children to do chores takes far more work and effort than if you were to just do the job yourself in the first place. I have a sneaking suspicion this is why so few moms really train their kids well.

Nope, lightening your load is not sufficient motivation. You're going to be discouraged if it is.

Eventually, of course, you'll have a lighter load, but that day is a little into the future, I'm sorry to say.

The real issue is to train them in skills they will need no matter their lot in life, career choices, and economic situation. Everyone needs to learn how to do basic household stuff. Everyone needs to clean up after themselves. Everyone needs the skills related to taking on age appropriate responsibilities.

Many children don't understand this.

Many parents don't either.

Chores are *not* about lightening your load as a mother.

Chores are about training our children.

Any other view of chores will leave you frustrated and discouraged, because your load is about to become temporarily heavier.

My oldest daughter had a brainstorm in this area a few months ago. We've been taking college level classes together through Faith Bible Institute, and the instructor was teaching out of Ephesians 4, where Paul discusses the real duty of pastors is to train church members for the work of the ministry. The instructor mentioned that this doesn't get done very often because it's easier to do it yourself. He even joked about how many people think a pastor is 'lazy' if he's trying to train church members to do what many think is supposed to be "his job", when the opposite is true, as it takes more effort to train someone than to just do it yourself.

> *Chores are not about lightening your load as a mother.*
>
> *Chores are about training our children.*

I could relate to that sentiment. It's so much easier to do something yourself than to take the time to train someone else to do it. Many times I've done a job myself because it was simply too overwhelming or frustrating to try to work with someone else at the moment.

"Now I get it!" Ruth said to me later.

"What?" I wondered

"Well, it's the same thing with you teaching us how to cook and clean and stuff. You had me teach Isobel how to do something recently, and I was ready to throttle her because she wasn't getting it, so I did it myself. But the point wasn't for the job to be done right the first time, or for me to have less work, but for her to learn..."

"Right," I said. I wanted her to learn as much as I wanted the chores done.

"So, you probably wanted to throttle me when you were teaching me how to do all of this stuff too?" she ventured.

"Uh....yes. A few times. Okay. Most days. It's not easy."

"No, it's not. I get that now, Mom. At first I used to think you wanted me to do stuff so you didn't have to, and that it was easier for me to do it. Quite the opposite, huh?"

"It is!"

The Long Haul

Training your children in chores is more like a long term investment than anything else. You can teach them things a dozen times, and still have to remind them.

When it comes to any aspect of child rearing, we need to have a long term vision for what we're hoping to achieve. We need long term goals to aim at.

We may all know, on some level anyway, that our children are not going to stay children for long. One day, Lord willing, they are going to be adults with households and children of their own.

I view my job as a mom right now as giving them the practical training tools for that likely future. I want to prepare them as best as I can for adulthood in every area I can. I wrote one of my other books, *Quiet Times in Loud Households* (available as paperback or for Kindle), to help parents in training their children spiritually. There are other books by other authors that go into more detail in child rearing and training for other areas. The point is, I want to help them mature spiritually, emotionally, physically, in work ethic, and in relationships.

Take some time to write out long term goals you'd like your children to know before adulthood, so you have something to shoot for.

During those days when I ask three times for the floor to be swept, I try to keep my eyes there – on the long term goal – instead of the short term results. Keep in mind what you're training them for and why.

You may find it helpful, as I did, to take some time to write out long term goals you'd like your children to know before adulthood, so you have something to shoot for.

3
Beyond the Chore Chart

If you're like me, you probably decided to start "training" your children to help out around the house by dividing up chores and deciding who is going to do what. Up on the wall, a fresh, new chore chart is hung. Every task in the household is accounted for.

The problem is, none of it gets done, at least not consistently.

> *Up on the wall, a fresh, new chore chart is hung. Every task in the household is accounted for. The problem is, none of it gets done, at least not consistently.*

Looking to some simple way to make our desires come true (in this case, a cleaner house and cheerfully helpful children) is human nature I think. We do this in so many areas of life: weight loss, relationships, budgets...

We all want a magic fix, and it isn't coming. I'm sorry to break that news to you.

As a young mom, this was a pressing need. At one point, if you do the math, I had four children ages five and under, and I was pregnant with my fifth.

This was truly a low point in my life, as a mom, because I felt really frustrated, exhausted and overwhelmed by life.

As I said earlier, I'm hardly super mom or the perfect homemaker, and keeping things clean is hard work for me.

Keeping things clean while pregnant in a house full of babies, toddlers, and preschoolers was impossible. Or so it seemed at the time.

Add to that, while six months' pregnant, I tripped and fell

down the stairs, breaking my foot and collar bone, and going onto bed rest. A few weeks later, I had to go back to the doctor to have my cast fixed. I had wore a hole in it. Is there any woman on bed rest with young children able to stay in bed?

I saw a magazine in the store around this time, and on the cover an article said, "How we trained our children to be helpers."

Ah, I need that, I thought to myself.

What mom doesn't?

Naturally I bought myself a copy of that magazine. The article had nothing practical in it. The mom writing the article was selling her chore chart software, which I also foolishly bought.

Every failed attempt to get my children to work seemed to be started with, "I know what I need! A new chore chart!"

A friend of mine often teases that I have codependency issues with office supply stores. Most projects or new ideas start with a trip to the local office supply store.

Every failed attempt to get my children to work seemed to be started with, "I know what I need! A new chore chart!"

I do the same thing for organizing myself. I long for order and to be organized. So, what do I do? I invest time or money (or both) into plans, charts, self-help books, planners, planner pages, and methods. The problem is, none of it works.

Why?

Because the real issue isn't that I've not found the perfect planner (or chore chart) yet. The real issue is disciplining myself.

Now, if all of the charts and planning in the world doesn't turn non-super moms like us into neatniks, how do we expect a simple planner or chore chart to turn our kids into helpers?

This is not to say that charts don't have their place. They do. We have a chores' chart hanging in the dining room and use it. However, getting kids to help is not about slapping a chores' chart on the wall and hoping they catch on, even with the promise of a sticker or some other treat.

Most children just don't roll that way, I'm sorry to say.

Until they are about eight or nine years old, and maybe even after that, they need to be reminded, encouraged, shown, taught, trained, and directed as to what to do very specifically. Younger children need you to be guiding and directing them, so that being able to know what to do soon becomes second nature, a habit developed. In this regard, I appreciate Charlotte Mason's philosophy on training children in good habits from a young age. We all, adults and children alike, need to form better habits in every area of life, don't we?

Tonight, one of my daughters, age fifteen, was scheduled to clean up the kitchen. Sadly, Tuesday is also a favorite TV night. I reminded her after dishes were done (by other siblings) but before her favorite show. As I came in to make some popcorn, She was just mopping up. Everything looked fantastic.

Did she do all of that because the chore chart said, "Today is your day to clean the kitchen?"

No.

A mom can't say, "Clean the kitchen" to a younger or untrained child, and expect it to be clean from floor to ceiling, with the faucets glistening and the floor spotless.

A mom can't say, "Clean the kitchen" to a younger or untrained child, and expect it to be clean from floor to ceiling, with the faucets glistening and the floor spotless. What does that even mean, to clean the kitchen? I am sure that even you and I have two different ideas as to what constitutes a "clean kitchen". No, a mom will be more effective if she shows them, multiple times, what it means to clean the kitchen, start to finish. Make it a habit.

Several years ago, I started training her. We worked together over and over again until a habit was formed. *That's* how you get a fifteen year old to make your kitchen shine in under an hour.

Of course, the pressure of not missing her favorite TV show also helps.

Now when I say to one of my older kids, "Could you please clean up the kitchen?" they know what I mean (mostly). Sometimes they'll ask, "A deep clean or just picking up?" because my children know that I don't always mean to empty out all of the cupboards and wipe down shelves.

Some of them are still learning. I just had a training moment with my two younger daughters who were cleaning the kitchen up and thought it better to start from the floor and work their way up. This situation gave me the opportunity to reinforce the habit of how to clean up the kitchen best. We went back over the whole idea of cleaning top to bottom, and doing the floor last. They saw why when they saw how bad the floor looked after cleaning off the counter where we were making pizza earlier that day.

4

Harness the Childlike Enthusiasm

One of the most fun things about a toddler is their enthusiasm. For the most part, they have very little fear of failure, unless they've been taught it. If someone could just bottle up "Essence of Energy of Toddler" and sell it, they'd make a fortune.

If someone could just bottle up "Essence of Energy of Toddler" and sell it, they'd make a fortune.

Toddlers have such a willingness to help too.

When my children were that age, they all wanted to help. They offered help all the time. They sometimes even butted in with their help even when I said no.

The problem was, they were, most of the time, of very little *real* help. Their "help" tended to make any task take twice as long while looking half as good. Those of you reading this with very young children probably can relate. Little ones have no idea how *unhelpful* they are being sometimes.

This desire to help that a young child or toddler has needs to be harnessed now. If you wait until they are of an age to be really helpful to your standards, then you will find them less willing to be your helper. Sure, a 3 year old doesn't do a perfect job setting a table, but she loves to help *right now,* and will be encouraged if you let her help.

By working alongside her, and helping her, over time you'll not only encourage her, but you'll slowly teach and train her how to do the chore better.

One of my favorite memories from my childhood was when

we were painting the outside of the house and garage. I wanted to paint. I actually remember painting the garage, and being a big help. Later, looking at slides shortly after we were married, I found out that actually I had been given a bucket of water and a huge paint brush to "paint" with. Even though I apparently didn't really paint, I remember feeling so proud of being a helper during that family project. To this day, painting is one of my favorite household tasks.

As I've worked on this book, I've talked with my children about their own memories of training. I asked each of them, "Do you remember when I started to train to you work on chores? What do you remember?"

All of them, separately, without hearing the others' answer, said the same thing.

"I don't remember ever *not* being your helper. I just always was there, working with you, and then around eight or so, I worked more on my own or with my brother or sisters."

Letting your little one be mommy's helper isn't always going to be possible every minute of every day, but letting them work with you as much as you can is well worth the time you invest in them.

I know all too well that I didn't always *willingly* accept their help. There were some days when I just wanted to be in the zone by myself, standing at the kitchen sink, singing along to Keith Green all by myself, without a preschooler talking my ear off. But for the most part, I tried to work with them as much as my sanity would allow.

Letting your little one be mommy's helper isn't always going to be possible every minute of every day, but letting them work with you as much as you can is well worth the time you invest in them.

5

Inconveniencing Yourself Today for Helpers Tomorrow

Obviously, doing housework yourself is far easier than doing it with a toddler, preschooler, or other child "helping" you. *Far easier.*

Training children to work when they are younger is more valuable to you, long term, than the "help" they are providing.

I'd like to encourage you, though, to inconvenience yourself today for the blessings tomorrow. I can assure you, they are well worth it.

No one will argue that training children to work when they are younger is more valuable to you, long term, than the "help" they are providing, because at this training level they are taking way more time than it would cost you to just do it yourself. Every mom knows, it is easier to just do it yourself many times. I have been tempted to just do a job myself, and I have done just that often. However, the more you work with them, especially when you are not in a time crunch, the better off you and your children will be in the long term.

As I said, this is not always feasible 365 days a year. In reality we can't do this each and every time. There's those days when standing at the sink doing dishes is a sort of mellow time alone with my own thoughts. Ditto for folding laundry or any number of other jobs. There are those days when someone is coming over in an hour and you plop them down in front of *Mary Poppins* while you clean up for company.

Although the days of training toddlers is past for me, I'm in a new season of life where I have had to practice this principle in a different way.

Right now, I'm in that stage of life where we are training our two oldest for driving. They both took driver's ed last year, but now they have to drive with their parents to practice for the road test, which in our state is quite strict.

My husband had a brilliant idea for how to get all of their driving time in. His brilliant idea was for them to come with me each time I go shopping. He drives with them on Saturday mornings, but due to his work schedule, the bulk of the driving falls to me.

There was one problem with that plan though. My weekly grocery trip is some time to get out of the house for two hours, and regroup a little bit, coming back refreshed.

Now, instead of chilling out, I was stressing out. I spend my drive to the grocery stores screaming, "LOOK OUT!" or "No, I said turn right not left!" or the oft-repeated "Don't forget your turn signal!"

I freely admit it: I'm not very good with this driver's ed thing.

Yes, they need to practice driving, but I can't do that every week, or I go a little batty. My time to relax gets invaded with an extremely stressful activity: driving with teenagers. In traffic. Potentially killing or maiming others or ourselves with one minor mistake.

As much as is possible though, we need to drive with the teens. They are never going to become confident, safe drivers if they never get the chance to practice what they've learned, under my supervision and guidance. Most Thursdays, it's far more stressful than just driving myself, but it's more beneficial to them in the long run.

While we may find a toddler's "help" far more stressful than simply doing the job ourselves, in the long run it is far more beneficial to both of us to let them help as often as we can.

In the same way, as much as is possible, we need to work alongside our little ones, and allow them to work alongside of us. While we may find a toddler's "help" far more stressful than simply doing the job ourselves, in the long run it is far more beneficial to both of us to let them help as often as we can.

On a recent shopping trip, I found myself realizing that my daughter had become a far more confident driver. She remembered turn signals. She didn't slam on the brakes to stop at the last minute for red lights. She seemed relaxed. She even had a better sense of direction than normal. Shortly after this manuscript was sent to the editors, she passed her road test.

I guess that's the point of requiring so many hours of driving with your parents before you can get your "real" license. Repetition and practice help you to become more comfortable with the task at hand.

You'll notice this with chores as well. Long before we turn our children loose with a charge to do a chore themselves, we have to inconvenience ourselves, logging in those training hours with them. The more you allow your children to help you while they are still young enough for their "help" to be more work than help, the better off you will be in the long run. One day you'll notice something different. The change may be subtle. But you'll see your child doing a better job, and even noticing when something needs to be done.

6
Lowering Your Standards Temporarily

W hen I worked in a donut shop, we used to train newbies during the slow parts of the day.

Now, finishing and decorating donuts wasn't rocket science. We were just adding the fillings, and dusting them with powdered sugar. But, we weren't about to let the new girl try to keep up during the busiest part of day, when the customers were all trying to get their morning cup of coffee and donut before work.

> *Mistakes are part of the learning process.*

Newbies make mistakes, and newbies don't make everything perfect right away. Sometimes they have to be taught only a small part of the job at a time, and slowly grow into it, while you're training them.

One of the hardest parts for the trainer is encouraging the trainee even when the job isn't quite up to snuff, but you can see they really are trying their best.

Mistakes are part of the learning process.

While we are training our children to be better helpers in our homes, we don't want to discourage them with standards set too high, just as we don't want to set the bar too low either. We don't want to hold them to some crazy perfectionism that they couldn't hope to achieve on their skill level.

Overlooking a job done to the best of their ability, when it is not up to your standard, is also quite difficult to do.

As with driving with my children, which I talked about in the last chapter, I had to keep in mind that they were still learning. That's why it's called a *learner's permit*. That's why they are supposed to drive all of those hours with their parents before moving to the next level: to learn. After seeing the reactions of other drivers to things my daughter and son did, I felt like I needed a "warning: new driver on board" sign for my car, so that people would have a little more grace and a little less road rage.

The whole point of the graduated driver's license in our state is that the state knows a *new* driver is not necessarily a *perfect* driver just because they could pass the driver education course. They need practice with an experienced driver to improve their skill and confidence.

In the same way, the point of this period of training your children isn't because we now expect them to be doing housework like a pro cleaning lady.

No. Training is to bring them, at their pace and according to their abilities, up to snuff.

Training is to bring them, at their pace and according to their abilities, up to snuff.

There's going to be some time between starting the training and the day when each of your children can do a fantastic job to your specifications.

The balancing act, I've found, is between helping children who want to do the minimum amount of work learn to work harder, and strive to do better, and on the flip side, helping those children who are comparing their skills with yours not be discouraged from even trying. Different children have different personalities.

I teach art once per week at a small private school. I create drawing lessons that are step by step for the kids to follow along with me. One little girl is always exasperated.

"Mrs. Eddy, how can you draw that good? Mine doesn't look as good as yours."

Well, the point of the art class, I try to tell her, is not for her to draw just like me. I tease her that if she drew just like me, she'd be teaching the class, instead of taking the class. With this kind of child, I have to work harder at encouraging her and praising what she is able to do. With other kids, they need more of a proverbial "nudge" in the right direction, repeatedly, to push them to do their best, not just go through the motions.

I know it's hard. I find it *very* hard. Relaxing a little bit when things are not exactly how you want them will be far more productive to a child willing to help, especially if they did their best, than if you hold them to a much higher standard.

When the children were younger, I let one of my daughters clean up the bathroom sink and counter top area all by herself. She wanted to do it. She was so proud when she came and said it was done, and she was so pleased with herself. I looked at it and was a little disappointed. She didn't do everything I wanted her to. I went in and "fixed it". I wasn't mad or anything. I just grabbed a rag and polished up the faucet, which had drip stains all over it. As I turned around, I saw the absolute hurt look on her face.

"Sorry. I tried, mommy," she said.

"No, no you did a great job. I just needed to fix a little...."

At that point I remembered that this was something that discouraged me from even wanting to try after a while.

I realized that encouraging my daughter in giving this task her best effort was far more important than a few spots on a faucet. I could always remind her how I wanted it done later, and I could always polish it after she walked away. After all for a seven year old, she did quite good in only forgetting one small thing! I didn't want to throw a wet blanket on her enthusiasm.

On the other hand, there are those children who try to figure out what the bare minimum requirement is, and push it to the limits.

On the other hand, there are those children who try to figure out what the bare minimum requirement is, and push it to the limits. If they're playing outside, and you tell them to go no further than the end of the driveway, they'll plant themselves right there, at the end of the driveway, and press their luck to see how far over the edge they can go before you do something. If you have them do the dishes, they'll "forget" to drain off the drain board (a common issue in our house).

The trick is figuring out which they need: the encouragement or the nudge.

Having Standards & Putting Forth the Effort

When I'm talking about relaxing our standards while we're still training our children, I'm not meaning to just give up on having any standards of housework. Please don't misunderstand.

I don't see much point in doing a job (or having someone else do a job) if it's not done right. Right?

What I am getting at here is to have some grace during the training time. You're dealing with *children*. Children who may not have ever done this task before. Learning takes time, and for some children it takes longer than others. Kids have differences in development of vision, coordination, the ability to understand verbal instructions, and so forth.

What I look for most with my own kids is more attitude than outcome, especially when starting out.

The trick is figuring out which they need: the encouragement or the nudge.

Did she do her best?

Did she work hard?

Did she try or did she just haphazardly finish the job at the bare minimum so she could go out and play?

When a child tries hard, even if the job isn't exactly up to par, I know I can always help that child do the job better next time. The next time she is to do the chore, I can always say, "Oh, let's do this together this time." That way I can try to reinforce how I want the chore done. I still try to praise that child, because I want her to be encouraged and excited to help out again. Mistakes happen, and I can live with those. Bad attitudes, laziness, and being afraid to even try, I can't live with.

I don't know about you, but as an adult, I don't always win. I don't always succeed. But I have tried to always try, even when failure is a possibility.

There's too many adults in this world around us afraid to try anything, because they have such a strong fear of failure. I want my kids to see that failure is only bad if it stops you from trying again.

As we train our children to be helpers, we want to help remove some of that fear of failure for them. This isn't just *chores*. This is *life*.

7
Cleaning Up Naturally

I didn't think much about my cleaning supplies until I had an overactive toddler who knew how to overrule any child safety device faster than I could. She was into everything. She could unlock anything. She even tried (successfully) to use hand tools she got into. People had a hard time believing the stories we told about this little toddler we had, who my husband nicknamed "Baby Macguyver" (from the 80's TV show).

One day, I took a quick shower while she was sleeping (or so I thought), only to come out, not 10 minutes later, to find that she had gotten out of her crib, into a locked cupboard, spilled a 25 pound bag of oats I just bought, and a gallon of honey, and she had touched every surface in the house with hands covered in the goo, which later hardened into a substance similar to concrete.

With a child like that, I couldn't risk there being any dangerous chemicals, even under lock and key. She was far too resourceful. Any mom who has had this kind of child knows, some children can get into anything and everything if you only turn your back for a few seconds.

Child safety locks and devices aren't always foolproof protection, and so we need to be careful with what chemicals we bring into our homes.

This becomes even more important as we start to teach our children how to help clean up around the house. A very young child that was allowed to use a spray bottle to help momma may decide, one day when you aren't looking for about three seconds, to grab the bottle and start "helping". The safer the mixture in our spray bottle, the safer our child will be.

Safe cleaning agents? *Yes, ma'am!*

First of all, many cleaners are now coming out with safer, more environmentally friendly, and all natural cleaners, simply because of public demand. Obviously anything that can clean up a spill on a stove is still not a toy to be played around with, and children need supervision when using cleaning supplies (even natural ones). Anything that makes our homes safer is a good thing.

There are also many home made recipes for all natural cleaners.

I have found the absolute best, all purpose cleaner around is actually White Vinegar. I fill a spray bottle half way with vinegar and half way with water, and this mixture cleans pretty much anything and everything, including hard water stains around my faucets. It's amazing!

Another safe and effective cleaner I only recently started using is a mixture of Vinegar, Dawn Dish Soap and Water. Mix 1 part Vinegar, 1 part blue Dawn brand Dish Soap, and 2 parts of water. This is really effective in cleaning my stove top, and pretty much anything else.

Child safety locks and devices aren't always foolproof protection, and so we need to be careful with what chemicals we bring into our homes.

I was particularly nervous about abrasive cleaners, because around the time that my daughter was a toddler, a child in our area had swallowed some kind of abrasive cleaner, and was horribly scarred. The poor toddler nearly died. Having a toddler who would and could get into pretty much anything, I knew just how easily that could have happened in our home, and it terrified me.

An older lady at my church shared with me that she used Baking Soda to clean anything that needed an abrasive cleaner. I still use Baking Soda today. Bonus: it's cheaper too!

There are lots of websites available out there with far more extensive instructions and recipes for safe and effective homemade cleaners that you can use in your home, so that's all I'll say about that. You'll be amazed at how many inexpensive everyday ingredients can be used to keep your house clean.

8
Picking Up
Personal Responsibility

Where does chores training start? And when should it start? Chores' training starts simply with putting away toys.

As soon as a child is able to dump the toys from the toy box, they can be playfully taught that the flow of toys can go both ways. The same toys that they dumped can be made to jump back into the box or bin.

I have found the absolute best, all purpose cleaner around is actually White Vinegar.

As with most things, I always tried to make a game of it, as this seemed to make it stick better. Games go over well with the young ones.

There are some tips that will help you with this process:

Make it a habit of having your child put away their toys before moving onto a new activity. If they're young, obviously they'll do it with you (with you doing most of the work). But, the point is to build a habit. We want a habit that says, "Before I move to the next project, I need to clean up this one".

Call "picking up" something cute, based on whatever they are into at the moment:

"Quick, let's get the toys into the cave [toy box] before the dragon gets them!"

"Okay, little squirrels, before lunch, we need to gather up all of these nuts [toys] and put them into the nest [toy box]!"

...you get the picture. You know what they're into. Be creative.

Store toys in a way that is easy for a young one to take them out and put them back again. Usually, we had a large toy bucket for different kinds of toys – a bucket for blocks, a bucket for Legos, a box of doll stuff. Any game or anything else with lots of small pieces was kept up and away so we didn't break anything or lose pieces. Not only that, with so many little ones around, small parts pose a choking hazard.

Less is more with toys. I know, I know. This is not easy to enforce when you have enthusiastic grandparents buying toys. I have found that packing up some toys seasonally and rotating them every few months is like Christmas all over again. There is less of an overwhelming feeling regarding all of those toys, and it becomes easier to clean the room or play area. Plus, children enjoy the thrill of seeing "new" toys that they haven't seen for a while.

As soon as a child is able to dump the toys from the toy box, they can be taught that the same toys that they dumped can be made to jump back into the box.

Again this is one of those times where the job takes ten minutes when it could have taken thirty seconds, but the habit you're building in your children is well worth the nine minutes you're losing!

Part Two: Practical Training Tools

Introduction

This section is some advice on what kids can do at different ages and how to help them learn, how to work with them, etc. Most of it is based on my own experiences with my five children and also with my friends.

If you look online you'll see a great many web sites with chore charts listing age appropriate jobs for children to do. These are a great start, but again, without taking the time to do the job with them, and show them how to do it, most children aren't going to automatically understand what it means to vacuum the living room. Did you?

So, let's talk practical training tips in these different areas.

9
Toddlers and Preschoolers

I said it before, and I'll repeat myself.

Your most important task is not so much getting them to help you out. There isn't much mystery in signing up a toddler to help you. Toddlers tend to spend large parts of the day asking to help, or insisting on helping you out.

> *What toddlers and preschoolers lack in skill they'll make up for in enthusiasm and desire.*

No, your most important task at this age is to harness their enthusiasm, praise them and make them feel proud to help you out, even if you and I both know that they are about as helpful as the family cat.

What toddlers and preschoolers lack in skill they'll make up for in enthusiasm and desire. You have to love that.

What kinds of chores can a toddler and preschooler help out with?

- Folding washcloths into squares – in half, turn it, then fold in half again. I think most of my kids learned their colors while doing washcloths with me. I bought a cheap pack of washcloths all in Primary and Secondary colors. We used to name the colors as we folded them.

- Holding a dustpan for you. This one can get a little messy sometimes.

- They may be able to use a small broom and dustpan too.

- Picking up their toys
- Putting the silverware at the table next to each plate.
- Using a little watering can to water hardy plants in the garden.

All of my kids loved to dust at this age, too. Just give them a rag or a duster, and turn them loose.

10
Younger Elementary Age

Children grow so fast. You've probably noticed that yourself.

They don't stay toddlers and preschoolers for long. Soon, they are growing up and becoming little ladies and gentlemen. By the time they are in what I suppose we could call "early elementary age" (about ages 6-10, roughly), kids are a little more capable but still willing and eager to help out mommy, unless they've learned otherwise.

By the time they are about ages 6-10, kids are a little more capable but still willing and eager to help out mommy, unless they've learned otherwise.

What do I mean? Well, it depends on their peers.

We home school and have always home schooled, but peer pressure can still be there, in the form of friends, neighbors, relatives, and church.

I always had a super helpful child in the form of each of my children. I'm thankful to be so blessed, frankly. We hit a rough patch with one of our girls when she was about 8, when we allowed her to spend some time with a relative. She came home from the overnight activity telling me that since so and so didn't do chores, she didn't have to either. And so and so's mom says I'm a horrible mother for making her do chores.

On and on it went. I just stood there with my jaw on the floor. I'm not normally speechless, but in this case I was.

Completely and utterly speechless.

I had a completely different child with a really rotten attitude after less than 24 hours with a relative. After checking off that person from the list of people welcome to spend time with my kids, I nearly had to start from scratch helping her to see that I wasn't trying to be a mean mommy, but rather trying to help her to grow into a responsible adult.

Deep down, she knew I wasn't being a slave driver or ogre, and that in most cases we were working together in all of this "helping out", which a young child still needs, although less and less frequently. It took a few weeks worth of encouragement and reminders before I had my cheerfully helpful daughter back.

A Little Boot Camp for Chores

When my children were getting to be of the ages where they could do a little more and take a little more responsibility with certain things, such as making their beds each morning without help, I would set up what we called a little "boot camp".

This was actually a sarcastic name we gave it, because that same relative who felt I was too strict with my children said my house was like boot camp. It really wasn't. We have a lot of fun. We just had two things they didn't in their house:

You don't just start off your first piano lesson playing "Linus and Lucy". You start off by finding the right keys, and practicing to the point that your fingers can find those keys automatically.

1. We had rules

2. We had chores

Many hands make light work, and all that. Now that my children are all in their teens but not acting like "teenagers" she has come around a little more to my way of thinking.

Anyway, onto the topic of boot camp. Essentially we'd have "boot camp" about any number of things we were teaching them.

Habit-Forming

The idea is similar to learning to play an instrument.

You don't just start off your first piano lesson playing "Linus and Lucy". You start off by finding the right keys, and practicing to the point that your fingers can find those keys automatically. Habitually. Without even thinking about it. I've only had a few years of piano, but I can still remember those basics because they are now hard-wired into me. My hands automatically go into position near middle C when I'm near a keyboard even though I have no raw musical talent whatsoever.

That's the idea.

It works the same with pretty much anything: learning a foreign language, learning a sport, learning to knit, learning to sew, learning some other skill, learning math facts, learning to read.

Think about it for a moment. Do you think of phonics rules as you read? Probably not, unless you're reading something way above your reading level. It's automatic for you now, from practice.

There are some things that we want to be automatic, and those good habits get that way from practice, too.

Studies have shown that it takes about 21 days to form a habit. If you can do something regularly for 21 days, you'll have formed a habit that will not be easily broken. You can also apply this to anything in life.

So, we need to work on something consistently for 21 days, in order for us to form a lasting habit in our children. We usually will do one thing at a time, and work on it until we have it right, then add some other task.

If you can do something regularly for 21 days, you'll have formed a habit that will not be easily broken.

Hopefully, your children are already in the habit of cleaning up after themselves when playing with toys. Otherwise that would be the best place to start.

As you probably realized, that's going to be a lot more on you than on the kids at first. You, as mom, will need to remember to remind them to pick up before they move onto the next thing. For me, this was always the hardest part, because, as I've said, I'm not naturally the most organized or disciplined person on the planet.

Note to Self

Instead, I realized that the easiest way for me to remember to do this was to leave myself little notes where I'd see them. I left notes to myself (and still do) in places such as on the Fridge, or near the sink where I washed dishes, on the door to the bathroom, or right above the toilet paper in the potty. Incidentally, I find hanging up memory verses to learn or things to memorize near the toilet to be the best place. We even have SAT questions and answers there.

If you're among the born organized, that may seem really silly. My mom and some friends sure got a laugh that I had to remind myself to remind the kids to pick up toys when they were younger. But, the important thing is, it worked. Within a week and a half, it had become a pretty regular habit for me.

Don't just say, "Well I have this planner book here. I'll write it down in there." If you're not the most organized person on the planet either, there's a better than good chance that you don't even remember to look in your planner.

How do I know?

Because that's happened to me more than once. Planners only work when you open them and look inside.

Bed Making Fun

We usually started off with having a rather fun "training session" for bed making.

The next best step for training your children, I think, is to make your bed each morning. A made bed seems to make the room look neater, and gives you one less thing to do at the end of the day.

We usually started off with having a rather fun "training session" for bed making. When I say fun, I mean it too. I tried to make these kinds of things into a game, family fun time, or whatever else you wanted to call it.

I feel I need to stress that right off the bat, because I don't want anyone reading how we did this and assuming that I was being a mean momma.

So, let me start by saying, get the radio going. Pop in some fun, upbeat song of some sort. This can be pretty fun and pretty silly. I can assure you, it also sticks with them when you have a good time learning it.

If you grew up in the 70s and 80s, you probably remember a lot of math, history and grammar from the *Schoolhouse Rock Videos* (which can be purchased, by the way, on DVD at Amazon.com, or even viewed on YouTube.com).

Why? *Music and fun.*

In my 12th grade Government class, I could hear all of my classmates humming the tune to the song with the Preamble to the Constitution while we took the final exam. I can still quote the Preamble using that song. You probably can too. You learned something while having fun and singing a song.

They will be making their beds for the rest of their lives. Let's associate it with some fun, laughter, and family time, right?

I started off by showing them a few steps that we tried to remember. Since we were dealing with pretty young elementary age kids, including one that sometimes had accidents during sleep, the first step was to feel the bed to make sure it was dry. If it's wet, it goes in the wash, and they were to come get me.

Then I pulled everything off the bed, and showed them step by step how to make it, several times. Each time I made a point of saying the step in an easy to understand and easy to remember way. Again, if you need to, use things that they are really into at the time (trains, dinosaurs, dragons, puppies – whatever works).

We also had races to see who could get theirs made fastest, and accurately of course.

After doing that a few times, I pulled it off, and had the child do it, with me helping them. We did this a few times too.

Then I had them do it by themselves.

The whole time, we were singing, laughing, and at times falling down into piles of blankets on the floor.

If there were two children in the same room learning at the same time, we also had races to see who could get theirs made fastest, and accurately of course.

We had a few different times when we did this particular activity to really get them to know how to do it. Now that about 10 or more years has passed since we did this, I do find that periodically I need to go back and do bed checks, to make sure they make their beds in the morning. Sometimes things lapse. For the most part, this has stuck with them, though.

Later, I've added other things to this, such as how to put the fitted sheet on, or "If it's the 2nd or 4th Monday, then it's your day to wash your bed linens." Those are more advanced, for older kids though. I found my younger ones had a really hard time with fitted sheets, so I dropped that requirement until they were a little older (8-10 and up).

I used a similar approach with many of the chores I wanted them to learn to do, although obviously with most other things you can't "undo" and "redo" something in the same way you can undo and redo making a bed. The repetition over a few days with other chores can help them remember how to do it. Doing it a certain way each time, step by step, will help both you and the kids do things right each time too. Again, this was a help to both me and the kids, since I was in desperate need of organizational help myself.

This had the added benefit of forcing me into some more disciplined living while training them. Through helping my children learn to do chores, I became far more organized than I ever was before.

Laundry

Doing chores a certain way each time, step by step, will help both you and the kids do things right each time too.

Clothing is another area that causes messiness in most kids' rooms. We can teach them some basics to get this under control too.

Usually around this age, I would start to have the children put their own laundry away (after I folded it or hung it on a hanger). I would bring it into their rooms, and together, we'd put it into the right drawers. I had little signs on their dresser drawers to know which drawer was for which kinds of items, which I simply taped there.

If at all possible, make sure that a child's dresser drawers are easily opened, so that they can help without struggling with the drawers. It's also a good idea to have a "catch" on the drawers (which most do now) so that the drawer doesn't easily pull all the way out (and land on toes).

I'd also like to point out a word of safety. A friend on Facebook lost her dear son about two years ago, when a heavy piece of furniture toppled over onto him. **Make sure furniture is fairly secure.** If necessary, use a cheap metal bracket (these are found in hardware stores, look like an "L", and cost around a dollar), some screws, and wall anchors, and secure bookshelves and anything else that may topple over, to your walls. After this incident, another friend gave each piece of furniture in her kids' rooms a good shake, and discovered a dresser tipped when grabbed by the top-front edge. We secured it to the wall with a bracket so that won't happen.

Having a laundry hamper or basket for dirty laundry in the room is also a great idea to help them clean up. This way, they can put dirty clothes into the hamper when they are done wearing them. I spent some time teaching them that socks, underwear, and shirts always went into the hamper, but skirts and pants could usually be worn again unless they were dirty. We had some "training" to build the habit of putting today's clothes into the hamper when changing into pajamas. I also spent time training them to put pajamas under their pillow in the morning after they get dressed and make their beds. There was a certain day of the week to put the pj's into the hamper.

In the kids' math textbook around this time, a few of them were learning how to read a calendar, and check off the days of the week. The teachers' guide had suggested having specific things for specific days to help reinforce the idea of different days. Regardless of your mode of education, whenever you help your child apply school work to things in the "real world" they will understand the lessons much better, and will likely learn more. Again, this also helped me to be more orderly, along with the kids!

A friend on Facebook lost her dear son about two years ago, when a heavy piece of furniture toppled over onto him. Make sure furniture is fairly secure.

The "Clean Laundry in the Hamper" Trick

I mentioned before that one of my "methods" of cleaning my room as a child – more gray hair for my poor momma – was to throw whatever clothing I left on the floor into the hamper, such that "cleaning my room" resulted in 3 days' worth of laundry for mom. No one needs to teach children to do this. They figure this little trick out very easily on their own.

So, how do you prevent it?

I found that having a sufficiently good penalty for doing this usually helped stop it. You know your children better than I do, so find something they enjoy to take away as a punishment for creating a certain amount of work for you. I am a big believer on having the "punishment" fit the "crime". That is, a real world consequence to go with whatever it was that they do wrong. When you do certain things in the "real world" certain other things happen. I want whatever consequence I gave to my children to reflect that. When you put non-dirty clothes into the wash because you're being lazy, you're creating x amount of work for me, and you're unnecessarily raising my water bill, electric bill (for the washer), gas bill (for the dryer) and the cost of detergent.

Sometimes, I would have them do chores equal to the time I was going to have to spend doing the extra laundry, or to skip an activity. Sometimes it was being grounded. The punishment really was based on what they were doing at the time, and I always tried to make it fit what they did wrong, based on their level of understanding. This works if it's not merely *punitive*, but *instructive*. You want them to learn something, not be "punished" for something. They also need to be old enough to understand this part of it, so this only works for older children whose understanding would make this work. In other words, a two year old may not learn from it the same way an eight year old would.

Later, I taught my children to do their own wash (everyone has a day of the week for their wash day) and this practice of cleaning up by throwing clean clothes into dirty laundry ended pretty quickly

Later, I taught my children to do their own wash (everyone has a day of the week for their wash day) and this practice of cleaning up by throwing clean clothes into dirty laundry ended pretty quickly. After all, everyone is quite particular about what is and is not supposed to be in "their" laundry. If extra stuff gets thrown in, most of my girls make a fuss about it. They have been very effective about policing themselves and each other.

Kitchen Helpers

Children can also help you out with some kitchen duties, although care needs to be taken. Safety must come first. There are many dangers in the kitchen, but when taught proper safety techniques, children really enjoy helping out mom in the kitchen.

A good starting point is setting the table. Young children can be taught to set the table properly at this age. One of the most effective ways to help them remember everything is to have place mats with a place-setting outline on them to follow as a guideline. These kinds of place mats can be found for sale at most stores, or you can make your own, and cover with clear or frosted contact paper.

I usually start off, again, with a training session, having them practice with each place setting at the table, to get it down pat.

I know when it comes to letting a younger child help with doing dishes and setting the table, many moms may be concerned about losing plates in the process. I am not a big fan of plastic plates, but with young children this can be a great temporary option, until they become more confident at least.

Using non-breakable plates at this point is easier than using your fine China dishes, of course, and safer for children until they get better with helping set the table. Most of these non-breakable plates can be found fairly inexpensively at the Dollar Store, Big Lots, or other discount stores. Sometimes you may even find them at garage sales and thrift stores. I've noticed that the ones sold near the picnic supplies tend to be cheaper than the ones near the children's department with cute characters on them. They also look a little more "adult".

One of the most effective ways to help them remember how to set the table, is to have place mats with a place-setting outline on them to follow as a guideline.

Young children can also help unload and sort silverware from the dishwasher. They may even be able to help put away other things from the dishwasher if the shelves are low enough. I usually had my young ones put away things whose shelves were within easy reach.

Many children love to cook with mom. Actually, most children love to do anything you're doing, and they love to do it with you.

I am more concerned about their safety though, so use your best judgment. There are many hazards in the kitchen (knives, hot surfaces, fire). I am very conscientious when it comes to allowing my children help in the kitchen, and I always try to put safety first. Later, I'll share with you a dozen simple kitchen safety rules we try to follow.

Baking Cookies

How many of us have happy memories of childhood associated with baking cookies either with our mom or our grandmother? I know I do. Sure, we all try to be more health conscious now, and that's good. But, don't dismiss the value of baking cookies from time to time with your kids.

I really think the real value of baking cookies with your children is not the *cookies* part.

Cookies aren't healthy. Who needs the extra fat and sugar? But the value isn't in what you're making. The value is time spent in the kitchen together. Baking cookies can be a great bonding moment for parent and child, as well as a stepping stone towards learning other cooking skills.

> *The real value of baking cookies with your children isn't in what you're making. The value is time spent in the kitchen together.*

When you're baking cookies, there are so many skills that a younger elementary child is being exposed to, that they are also learning about in their school work.

- Measurements (how to measure ingredients)
- Fractions (especially if you are doubling a recipe)
- Time (how long should these be in the oven?)
- Patterns (laying cookies on a cookie sheet in an orderly way)
- Temperature
- Eye-hand coordination (using cookie cutters)

The next time you bake something, bake it with them. They'll enjoy it, and you'll enjoy it too.

We are very into music in our house, so we always would pop in some good music, and sing and have a little party in the kitchen when baking together. Our neighbors probably think we're weirdos, but we tend to sing together with whatever we have on the radio all the time. And, lest you think we sound something like the Von Trapps, I can assure you that my singing abilities are slightly worse than my natural cleaning skills. No one sits in front of me in church for a reason, and I'll likely never be asked to sing a solo.

It doesn't detour me (or anyone else in the family) from listening to and badly singing along to music while we work. Try it sometime!

More Chores with Young Children

Other things a younger elementary child can do with some oversight by you:

- picking up after themselves
- holding a dustpan
- sweeping up
- using a vacuum
- feeding dogs or cats
- folding simple laundry (towels are a good place to start, and matching socks)
- dusting and wiping woodwork

Every child is an individual, so it's hard to give you too many specifics to apply to "all kids this age".

Just use your own best judgment. You know your children. See what they're capable of already, and go from there. Every child is very individual, so it's hard to give you too many specifics to apply to "all kids this age".

As you let your children work alongside you and help you with different tasks, you'll see better what they are interested in and gifted in, as well as what they are able to do.

11
"Go Clean Your Room!"

I t's one of those things every mom says to her child at one time or another.

"Go clean your room!"

Sometimes it was even conditional on my getting to do something fun.

Usually I'd stare at my room for a few minutes to try to figure out what exactly was wrong with my room just the way it was.

"You can play with little Susie up the street after you've cleaned your room," parents will often say. I've even caught myself saying it to my children.

When I'd hear, "Go clean your room!" I'd go into my room.

Usually I'd stare at my room for a few minutes to try to figure out what exactly was wrong with my room just the way it was. *What specifically is bugging mom about this room?* Once I could figure that out, I could fix it, and get on with life.

I'd look around.

"Let's see. These clothes are dirty...or are they clean? I don't know. I'll put them all in the hamper to be sure. This sweater I wear all the time, so I'll put it over my chair. No sense in hanging it in the closet...

"Onto my desk. Well, I'm working on a research report, so I need to leave this out, and this....so I'll put this into a pile with that...."

"If I put this book back on the shelf I'll forgot why I pulled it out, so I better put it in this pile on my desk...."

This is how the room became a *slightly tidier mess* than it was when I started. I would shuffle the mess around, give my mother enough laundry for three days, and still leave the room "messy" by mom's standards.

Why is the command to "Go clean your room!" so difficult for children (and even some adults)?

Well, think about it for a moment.

"Go clean your room!"

Pretty vague, isn't it?

What did you have in mind? What is bugging you the most about the room? Piles of paper? Piles of laundry? An unmade bed? Clutter? A half eaten peanut butter sandwich that is fossilizing on a plate under the clutter?

(For the record, eating in bedrooms is not allowed in this house for this reason -- memories of finding ancient leftovers when cleaning. It's a wonder my mom wasn't gray at 30)

I don't feel it's disobedience if a child doesn't know what is expected of them. You can't obey what you don't know.

I don't feel it's disobedience if a child doesn't know what is expected of them. You can't obey what you don't know.

Your children may find the room just fine. They know where everything is. I had piles on my desk (and still do), and knew what each of them was for. So they shuffle their stuff around for an acceptable amount of time, and think the job is done.

I'm going to propose a different method.

Working together and spending some time training them how to do a job very specifically. In other words, giving your children a sort of checklist to run down regarding chores, such as cleaning their rooms.

Now, again, I'm not (not not NOT) talking about making this into some horribly irritating and frustrating experience. I'm talking about some fun, lighthearted time spent together.

Young children of this age can help keep their rooms clean. This skill can be continually improved upon as they grow and mature. I find that as with making beds, if you find one thing to work on in their room (for example, putting away shoes, or emptying the trash, or leaving no papers lying haphazardly on the desk — whatever you see a need for), and work on that one at a time, you'll have them slowly learn how to care for their own rooms.

Just having the habit of making a bed and picking up toys when you're done with them will solve much of the messiness problem in most rooms.

12

Combating Clutter in Children's Rooms

One major issue with keeping anything clean and organized is that many of us have frankly too much stuff. Too much stuff translates into more things to shuffle around, keep orderly, clean regularly, and fill up our spaces. Even if you are diligent with cleaning, a room or even home with too much stuff will still look messy.

Clutter makes it frustrating for your kids when you tell them to "go clean your room", because they may not have enough room to put it all neatly away,

Many times, children have more toys and clothes than they know what to do with or can properly organize by themselves. This makes it frustrating for them when you tell them to "go clean your room", because they may not have enough room to put it all neatly away, but that problem may not be apparent to them. Kids may not see exactly what the stumbling block to a clean room really is.

In our house, we just recently did a major decluttering of the bedroom of my youngest two daughters, brought on by a repair project, and long overdue. One of the kids' rooms was perpetually messy, and excessive clutter was certainly to blame.

I had noticed the clutter in their room, and had asked them to go through it, under threat that I would one day go in there with a box of contractor-type garbage bags. They would spend a day going through their stuff, and give me a couple of small bags for the Thrift store. There would be a small improvement in the room, but the clutter was still overwhelming.

I knew in my heart what I had to do though. I had to go through it with them. I just didn't feel like it. It was too overwhelming, even for me.

I think it was also too overwhelming for them.

We finally got the opportunity to declutter the room when some plaster had started to crack on the wall. Living in a 110 year old house with lath and plaster walls, this is a fact of life. Leaving it be for too long would mean potentially risking the whole wall coming down (been there, done that). I figured, if we're going to patch it up, we'll do a super cheap fix up on the room while we were at it. So, after patching plaster, we decided to repaint, and to seal up the floor with a couple of coats of poly acrylic I had leftover in the basement.

We painted the room after the plaster patching as an incentive to empty the room and go through everything. It worked.

I want this part of my house clean, but I have to remember to respect that many of these things are theirs, and may have sentimental value attached.

I try to tread carefully when cleaning out one of my kids' rooms, especially now that they are older. I want this part of my house clean, but I have to remember to respect that many of these things are theirs, and may have sentimental value attached. There are gifts from friends and grandparents, mementos from field trips that look like junk to me, and so forth.

The contents of their tiny bedroom filled the ample upstairs hallway to the ceiling, the upstairs bathroom, part of my bedroom, and most of the entryway. My oldest daughter joked that we looked like we were auditioning for *Hoarders*. Going through it all took us longer than it did to paint walls and add a fresh couple of coats of poly to the floor.

There are some simple principles to keep in mind when decluttering your children's rooms that I've found work best, and keep the task from being too overwhelming.

Plan for Regular Intervals

Children grow out of clothing. They grow out of their shoes faster than we can keep up with sometimes. Children grow out of furniture. They can grow out of toys and games.

I frequently remind my children to bring me any clothing that doesn't fit, doesn't work for them, needs fixing, and so forth. I've given them some autonomy in this area, as they are all old enough to do their own laundry, and everyone has a scheduled day. I'll talk more about that later.

The reality is, I can remind them all I want, but most of the time, my children don't remember to bring these things to me. Instead, the white blouse from six years ago missing two buttons with the Kool Aid stain down the front is stuffed into the back of the closet. The shelf of shoes is overloaded with shoes that haven't fit in years. The desk has pens that stopped working a while ago.

When we decluttered the girls' room after not doing it for a while, I even found toys from ages ago, that we were able to bless others with.

When my children were younger, I would go through seasonally, and pull out the clothing for the season. Then I would check the size, the fit, and see what we might need to look for at the thrift store. At that time, I also would go through the room with them and look for anything else that needed to go or move on.

When my children were younger, I would go through seasonally, and pull out the clothing for the season.

This is a far easier task if you do it regularly, than if you do it only when the mess is driving you completely batty.

Plan regular times of the year to go through the rooms and give them a thorough cleaning and decluttering, with your children.

The Tools of the Trade

So, what is the best way to help declutter a child's room?

First of all, I find it easiest to have three laundry baskets or boxes to use, for quick sorting of clothes or other items. One basket was for putting things away that belonged elsewhere, one was for putting away in the room once we were done, and one was for dirty laundry we found when cleaning up.

I also find that garbage bags, especially contractor-type garbage bags (heavy duty) are very helpful for a large decluttering job. This will help you clean up any garbage more easily without a bag that rips open.

White (or other color) garbage bags are good for bagging up items to give away to the thrift store. I find that if I put clothing to give away into a regular garbage bag, someone somewhere along the lines gets confused and puts garbage in with the clothing, or clothing into the garbage. Having a different color is a good way to keep items to give away and items that are trash separate.

Large plastic storage totes are also very handy to use when decluttering, as I'll tell you below. Much of our clutter issues can be helped by putting away things we won't use for a few months into storage, such as storing away sweaters in Summertime.

Put Seasonal Stuff Away

White (or other color) garbage bags are good for bagging up items to give away to the thrift store.

A good place to start in tackling clutter in children's rooms is with the seasonal clutter. What I mean by that is, putting away any clothing (and decorations) that you only wear during certain seasons.

My theory is that I shouldn't be tripping over flip flops in January in Michigan. I shouldn't see a heavy winter coat on the back of your door in July, either. Stuff you're not going to use for six months just contributes to the clutter if you don't put it away. There's no reason to leave the Christmas-themed sweaters, dresses, and blouses to take up room in the small closet, when I could put them in a tote for next Christmas season.

I have a spot (as many families do I think) for totes and bins full of seasonal wear, that we change out every season. We don't always remember to do it though. ;) The first thing we did was pull out all summer clothing and toys and put them into storage, if possible.

The grandparents also love to give gifts, and some of those gifts have included decorations for the girls' rooms for different holidays. The kids feel the need to leave all of this out all the time. The result was perpetually tripping over a miniature Christmas tree in that little room. *Yes, a Christmas tree.* Putting that away, as well as all of the mini-bulb decor that goes with it, helped tremendously.

If It Doesn't Fit (or You Don't Love It), Bless Someone Else with It

This is pretty straightforward, or at least should be.

If it doesn't fit, it shouldn't be in your dresser or closet. We moms need to do that too, don't we? I have a few "maybe I'll fit into this again before it's out of style" dresses I should probably bless someone else with too, now that I think of it.

The same is true for anything that you have that fits, but you don't ever wear because you don't like it. I found that kids, like adults, sometimes hang onto things so as to not hurt the feelings of someone who gave it to them.

I have to tread super carefully in this regard. I am not someone who gets all sentimental about things. I know my weaknesses as "Slobalina". I know that too much clutter makes it that much harder to overcome my natural sloppiness. So I usually have no trouble pitching that which I don't love or which doesn't fit. My children and husband are not like this at all. They tend to be very emotionally tied to the sentimental value of these things.

> *Kids, like adults, sometimes hang onto things so as to not hurt the feelings of someone who gave it to them.*

As a mom, I have to respect that some things have meaning and value beyond the obvious. The rock on the desk looks, to me, like a rock. To my daughter, it's a memory of a field trip and a friend she met on that beautiful August day.

One exception to the "get rid of it if it doesn't fit or you don't love it" rule is anything that is part of a necessary uniform. Our kids sing in choir, and do all sorts of activities at church and camp. Most of the time, the girls need a white blouse and a black skirt for these things. My attitude has had to be, "Even if you don't love the only long black skirt I could find in your size at the time on short notice before the Christmas cantata, you're keeping it, until a suitable replacement can be found."

I don't just apply this to clothing either. If some "object" doesn't fit in the room, we need to get rid of it. This is true if we don't have a place for it, and especially if we don't have a "need" for it. As children grow up, and grow in size, some furniture just gets outgrown, including old desks, doll houses, and other items.

During our most recent decluttering adventure, we were able to bless another family with our old metal school desks, which no longer fit our very tall children.

Get Rid of (or Store) Duplicates

When we are battling clutter, sometimes we buy (or fetch from other parts of the house) duplicates of what we already have, but cannot find. Pencils, pens, boxes of tissue, dustpans, boxes of small garbage bags…

All of this translates to clutter.

Now if you've read my main blog at www.JoyfulMomma.com a bit or read some of my books (especially *Joyful Momma's Guide to Shopping and Cooking Frugally*), you'll note I am big on bulk buying and stocking up when things are on sale for a great deal. That's *not* what I'm talking about here. When you stock up on something due to a great deal, you don't unpack it all at once. You don't leave the bulk purchase laying out, in the way either. At least, you shouldn't.

In our house, we store the extras out of the way, so as to not clutter up the rest of the house.

Well, when you are decluttering a room and you find extras, you need to either get rid of it or put it away in the spot in your house where extras of that item are stored.

In this case, we had one particularly artistic child who had pencils everywhere. I actually filled a cleaning bucket with PENCILS I found. And so, extra pencils (and other office supplies) were put away for later into a common storage area. Ours is a drawer in the china cabinet. This is a good way to declutter your desk too.

Damaged (and Unfix-able) Items Go to the Curb

My dear husband Martin and I are great bargain hunters, and love thrift stores. I often buy damaged goods that I know I can fix.

But, when you can't fix an item, it's time to take it to the curb.

I'm talking about stains you can't get out, holes worn in the wrong spots, tears that are not simple seam repair, broken wood, cracked mirrors, hair elastics that have lost their elastic, broken barrettes, hair brushes and combs where the bristles have broken off...you get the picture.

One or two stained up clothes are good for painting and gardening activities, but get rid of anything you can't wear due to stains.

Being a crafty person, I usually clip off any cool buttons, and embellishments that I can realistically use on something else.

13

Cheap Organizational Ideas for Children's Rooms

I know that it's been said, "You can't organize clutter". This is true. *Sort of.*

Just buying organizational stuff isn't going to fix a clutter prob-

Just buying organizational stuff isn't going to fix a clutter problem.

lem. You need to go through the first four steps first, and just empty the space as much as possible of anything that is unnecessary or unwanted. Organizing all of your stuff when you have way too much of it isn't going to make a huge difference.

In the case of children's rooms especially, but also any room, there may be better ways to organize and set up the space without spending a lot of money. We just have to figure that out.

A simple solution, to give you an idea, was a simple old metal can used for a pencil cup for the pencil-hoarder. I had a lot of smaller cans from the tiny cans of tomato sauce that went on sale, and we set up smaller cans to be used for things like hair elastics and barrettes. We covered the cans with ribbons we had already. Some cans we painted.

I also noted that one kid wrote notes to herself on the wall. (I let her wash it all of and see why that drives me nuts). I had leftover chalkboard paint from a different project so I painted a 6 inch stripe of chalkboard on their wall. Now they can write on the wall all they want on the chalkboard area.

Another idea for helping keep the room neat was to buy an inexpensive over the door hanger. It had six hooks on it, and is made out of metal. This only cost $3 at the Dollar Store, but it has helped keep things neat. We also bought over the door organizers for shoes, which hangs up in the closet.

The best idea so far, though, and my favorite, is using hardback suitcases for under the bed storage. For years, we'd periodically buy those plastic organizers that have wheels, and usually crack from usage from children. I went to the Thrift Store hoping to find some organizational helps, and we found several hard suitcases, and two small cassette tape cases. The cassette tape cases can easily have the cassette tape organizer things pulled out of them. We glued felt inside of both boxes, and we decoupaged inside of another case. The suitcases had nice linings and their clasps worked well. Most "modern" suitcases with zippers that you find at the Thrift Store usually have broken zippers, or the zippers break easily. I'd avoid those.

A friend of mine uses a cute little "train case" suitcase for her daughter's doll stuff. Her daughter loves dragging around that suitcase with all her doll gear in it, and it's a wholly unique piece that looks nice in the room too, when not in active use. The fact that it cost about a dollar at the Thrift Store doesn't hurt.

My favorite "Thrift Store Organizing" idea is using hardback suitcases for under the bed storage, or other storage.

Suitcases are also good for storing grown up things too. I use several vintage suitcases (all unmatched) for my extra fabric and craft materials. If we ever get around to taking a vacation, we'll have plenty of luggage.

If you already have suitcases in your house that you don't use regularly, those can be put to use storing other items.

Those cookie tins that are tall and skinny, found around the holidays mostly it seems, are fantastic for storing paint brushes and sets of watercolors. Items like this are usually found in Thrift Stores for very cheap.

These are just a few ideas that I've found helpful for sorting out the little odds and ends in my kids' rooms. Look around the house with fresh eyes for items that might be re-purposed for better organization in other rooms.

14
Older Elementary

Something happens around age 8-10. Children really make huge leaps in ability and development. They aren't as uncoordinated as they were as very young children. They are more capable of doing many things. At this age, they are usually better able to help, but not always as eager.

The problem is one of attitude, most of the time. By this age, they've learned to associate housework and chores with a negative attitude. That is, they might view chores and housework as something to avoid at all costs. This can be learned by peers or by parents, or even by other adults around them.

Many parents run into problems with chores because they wait until around this age to give their children some chores to do, instead of really capitalizing on that enthusiasm and helpfulness when they are younger (and less able).

Does this mean it's impossible to start now? Thankfully, no. It's not impossible to start training children at this age, but it may be more difficult at the beginning.

Encouraging Helpfulness

My husband told me recently that he has memories from when he was this age, when his father told him he was going to have to start helping out around the house to "earn his keep a little". As you might imagine, that went over like a lead balloon, and eventually my in-laws gave up on trying to get their boys to help out much at all.

If mom wakes up one morning, decides she's had enough, and it's time for the children to help out, that doesn't mean her children will be equally motivated. Many moms have gotten to that point, composed a 20 point list of what their child needs to do before they can boot up their X-Box, only to be frustrated when no one "sees the light" and perform the chores on the list. After years of not requiring any chores or going about it *willy nilly*, there will either be a revolt in the house, or the kids will just ignore her until she gets off of the "cleaning kick" once more.

The key to getting helpful helpers, especially if you've not been encouraging that trait and praising little ones for their helpfulness, is not to turn chores into something to dread, but making them as enjoyable as possible.

As I wrote this book, and talked about its contents with my kids, they were all pretty unanimous. If you were to ask them, they'd tell you I brainwashed them from an early age into viewing housework as fun instead of work. You'll not hear too many 14 year olds telling their friends how much they like doing dishes. It's even stranger when you realize we don't have an automatic dishwasher. No, I have five organic dish washing units instead (my children).

Whenever we view what we have to do as a burden, it saps all of our energy to get it done.

As a child and teen, I viewed housework and chores as work. The housework that was being pawned off onto me was viewed as a burden. My parents conveyed that they were burdened with all of this work to do, and they needed me to help out to ease their burden.

I think choosing to view it as fun, and refer to it as fun, works better for me, personally. Whenever we view what we have to do as a burden, it saps all of our energy to get it done.

That doesn't mean you have to, right now, at this moment, view housework in general or a specific chore in particular as great fun. If you try to somehow convince your skeptical eight year old how much fun doing dishes is after watching you for years grumble about doing dishes, he's not going to buy it.

No, the best place to start is spending time together.

"Hey, Junior, come here for a bit. So, tell me about your day. Anything good happen? Oh, here. Can you wipe this plate dry and put it over there please? Thank you..." Spend some time with them. Let them talk to you about their interests or what they're reading right now, and one piece at a time, get them helping you.

When all is done, thank them for their help, and for how much it meant to you to get to do dishes with them. Be genuine about it.

If you've only been scolding, "Junior! I expect this bed to be made!" but you've not taught them how to make it properly (Junior could be standing there thinking... "uhhh...let's see...the sheet goes on the bottom, right?"), then maybe it's time to walk in one morning and say, "Hey, you want some help with that? Let me show you a trick that helps me...."

The way I see it, there are two main pitfalls we need to avoid in parenting.

There are many parents today who raise their children in such a way that the child thinks the whole world is there to serve them. This is obviously wrong, and the child is going to get a nasty surprise when they enter the proverbial "real world". But there are other parents on the opposite side of the spectrum who treat their children, especially in this area of chores, as if the kids are here to lighten the parents' load or ease their housework burden.

Spend some time with them. Let them talk to you about their interests or what they're reading right now, and one piece at a time, get them helping you.

I heard stories from every range of the spectrum when I started talking about finishing up this book on training your children to do chores. There were stories from adults who were frustrated that they never learned to work as children. Many of them related the difficulties of an added learning curve both in keeping a house clean but also in learning to work in general.

On the other side, I also heard stories from adults who didn't want to burden their children with chores because they felt they were overburdened with chores when they were younger. One friend told me that she remembers her mom constantly yelling at her and her sister, "I'm not your maid! You need to pull your share of the load around here." Every time her mom said that, she remembered thinking, "So does that mean we're your maids?" She was telling me that, now that she's a grown woman, she knows that's not what her mom meant at all. But, it's made her more cautious about the words she uses with her kids.

Thankfully, there's a third option.

That option is what I've been talking about. Working with your children. Working at their side. Enjoying their company while you both do the work. Displaying a good attitude about work, which we'll talk in greater depth about later.

Starting Small

As with a very young child, when trying to get an older child to start doing chores, you'll need to start off small, so as not to overwhelm them. Pick out specific things to train them to do, and to get them into the habit of doing it before moving onto the next item on the list. They need to spend time with you and work with you, while they learn how to work.

The proper motivation will also be of help here. Find out what will motivate them. I think that rewards can work well when starting out, and while they are still learning. Smaller rewards that would be meaningful to your child (you know them better than I) can help to motivate, especially when starting out. When we've done a big job, such

> *The proper motivation will also be of help here. Find out what will motivate them.*

as catching up on weeding the garden after two weeks of rain and hot weather (can you say Rain Forest?), I'll usually motivate with the promise of a trip to the Zoo or park when we're done.

Laundry

Children of this age can start to help out a little bit more with laundry, depending on their skills. As I said earlier, each of our children were assigned a different day to wash, dry, and fold their own laundry. This wasn't something we taught them all at once. We helped them to learn this step by step.

I started off by teaching them how to remove clothes from the washer, put them into the dryer, clean the dryer link from the lint screen, and turn the dryer on. I also taught them to bring the clean, dry laundry up from the basement. This seemed to us to be easier than starting off teaching them how to wash laundry.

Later, my kids were taught how to sort and wash laundry. For example, not putting a white shirt in with a load of colors or darks, and learning to always read care labels. I always supervised this for the first year or so. New washing machines are too expensive to just let the kids have at it. Every now and then I have to give out reminders about trying to stuff a week's worth of clothes into one load, especially for certain children.

After I began to train the youngest how to do laundry, I decided to assign each of us our day to do laundry. Monday is my oldest daughter's day, Tuesday is my son's day, and so forth. On Saturday, I do my own laundry, hubby's laundry, and any household laundry (towels, mostly).

We occasionally fall behind in this plan from time to time, mostly when we've had a bout of flu, or like during last summer's chicken pox outbreak. We called that chicken pox 2.0, since they had all had them as young children too. When that happens, we work together to get caught up, and then go back onto our weekly plan. Life seems so much more peaceful with that weekly plan in place.

After I began to train the youngest how to do laundry, I decided to assign each of us our day to do laundry.

I also showed them how to fold and hang up different pieces of laundry. As I said in the last section, we start off with towels, as those are easiest to fold. They are usually square or rectangle shaped, so they are a bit easier than the odd shape of a shirt. Hanging and folding laundry correctly helps us to save on ironing chores, which is probably my least favorite thing to do.

Teaching children how to iron clothes is also a good skill to know. Because hot irons can cause burns, not only from the surface, but also from the steam, this is a chore to judge based on the maturity and skill of the child. It's also one that I always do with extreme supervision, at least until my kids are older and are more confident.

In our house we don't iron too much. My motto is, "If it's not wash and wear, I don't wash it and I don't wear it." With that said, some ironing becomes necessary, especially with special outfits. When ironing is necessary, I use the occasion to show the kids how it's done, and to work with them on this skill.

Bathroom Duty

When it comes to cleaning the bathroom, this solves two problems, usually. Those issues are:

1. Cleaning the bathroom itself
2. Helping the kids to be more careful about spills, splashes, wet towels on the floor, and so forth.

If they have to clean it up, they tend to aim better, if you catch my meaning.

Around this age, I start to make them responsible for changing out the empty rolls of toilet paper on the holder, instead of just leaving the empty roll, and standing up the fresh roll on top. They also are usually made responsible for wiping up spills in sinks and on the floor, as well as a gentle wipe-down of the tub and shower area when they take showers or baths. Wiping down the tub right after your bath or shower makes the clean up a lot easier.

The Towel Police

When ironing is necessary, I use the occasion to show the kids how it's done, and to work with them on this skill.

An important issue to address with regards to cleaning the bathroom (and other rooms) is the importance of using the right rags.

I'm not sure if this is just my own children (and husband, for that matter) but my children seemed to think that any towel of "rag size" could be used to wash anything. I nearly died when I saw them using a dish cloth to wipe off the sink in the bathroom, and later found out that it was also used to wipe down the toilet too.

Gross.

They were a little confused, given that we do wash them after we're done cleaning. They assumed that this meant they were perfectly clean for use on dishes after going through the wash. Maybe they are. But, to me, it's just an unappetizing thought to wash dishes or anything else in the kitchen and dining room with rags that had been used just last week on the toilet.

By the time the kids were old enough for this level of helping out, the few towels I had received for my wedding were already falling apart anyway. I told my dear husband that what I wanted most for my anniversary that year was to be able to go buy new towels. In doing so, I bought what we could afford of course, but in certain colors for certain tasks. Black, gray, and black, gray, and white prints are all for kitchen and food surfaces. Greens, browns, and blues are all for the bathroom (hand towels, etc.). Rags are any towel that has an edge that I cut. In other words, don't use my hand towels as rags.

Color coordinating the towels has been a great help over these last several years, and teaching children (and husband) the difference between rags, dish cloths, dish towels, wash cloths and hand towels has kept me sane.

Obviously, towels are expensive, and just going out and buying towels in order to color coordinate is not in the budget of many of us (me included). There are some other ideas for helping your family tell the difference between the different towels for different uses.

Teaching children (and husband) the difference between rags, dish cloths, dish towels, wash cloths and hand towels has kept me sane.

Cutting "rags" in half, leaving a ragged edge, will help distinguish them from other towels.

Using a permanent marker, you may be able to color coordinate or put an initial on the tags of other towels ("DC" for Dish Cloth, "HT" for Hand Towel, and so forth).

Have a separate drawer or area for storing each kind of towel. Make sure rags are stored away from other towels to avoid confusion.

When buying cleaning sponges, which need to be replaced more frequently, buy different colors for different tasks. For example, yellow for the kitchen, blue for the bathroom. That way the sponge used to clean soap scum in the bathroom doesn't get used to clean your kitchen counter.

Dishes

With seven people in our house, and three meals a day, if we were at all lax about dishes for even a few hours, we'd have a sink full of them.

From a young age, my children have been helping out with

washing dishes, but by the time they are pre-teens, they are able to take on more responsibility in this area. As with other chores, I spend quite a bit of time showing them just how the job is done, and even more time working alongside them to make sure the job is done properly before just leaving them to it.

Let me reiterate my earlier comments about dish towels, dish cloths, and sponges. We don't want to potentially spread germs about by not having specific towels and rags for specific tasks. I also make sure to soak the dish washing sponges in bleach water every week, to make sure to keep them clean.

Exactly how you teach your children to wash dishes really depends on how you want them done. I found it easier to train them to use the dishwasher at first, but I still showed them how to wash dishes by hand too. I'm glad I did, because a few years ago, our dishwasher died, and finances have not allowed us to replace it.

I also wanted my children to know that "dishes" aren't done until the sink area is wiped off and the counters are wiped down too. Having the sink area looking nice helps the whole kitchen to look cleaner.

With seven people in our house, and three meals a day, if we were at all lax about dishes for even a few hours, we'd have a sink full of them.

Floors

Earlier, I mentioned having your very young children help you out with holding the dustpan and maybe even using a small whisk broom. Many young children love to help in that way.

By the time children are older, they can help sweep up floors, mop floors, and vacuum carpeting.

I've tried to help them out by reminding them that it's better to clean any room top to bottom, saving the floor for last. That way, if any dirt, dust, and debris lands on the floor, you don't have to redo the job. This is far less frustrating.

So, if I've asked the kids to clean the dining room, and one child is assigned the table, one is assigned the shelf, and another is assigned the floor (that's how we usually tackle a room, by the way), I always remind them, even now, that the person doing the floor should wait until everyone else is done, to save themselves some frustration.

Simple Cooking Tasks

A several years ago, back when my son was about ten years old, he was standing with me while I chatted with a friend at the store. My friend was saying that she buys frozen pancakes because she hates having to make pancakes for her son, who was sixteen when he wants a late night snack. This way he can heat them up for himself and his friends.

My son was standing next to me, and I knew what he was thinking. Judah piped up before I could stop him, and said, "But, if he's 16, why can't he just make pancakes?"

This was a little confusing for him because, since he was eight years old, he has made breakfast most mornings without being asked to. His specialty is pancakes.

It's better to clean any room top to bottom, saving the floor for last. That way, if any dirt, dust, and debris lands on the floor, you don't have to redo the job.

How did we even start getting him to make breakfast? It wasn't a goal I planned on, that's for sure.

I had started teaching him how to cook, and how to help me make pancakes. He and his older sister one day told my husband and I that they think it would be nice if we could have something "a little more significant" for breakfast in the morning, besides just oatmeal, yogurt, granola, and fruit.

My husband said, "That sounds wonderful! What will *you* be making?"

Well, they took that question quite seriously, and asked me to help them learn to make dishes like French Toast, Pancakes, and even Omelets. After some training, they caught on rather quickly.

Teaching a child to be careful in the kitchen, and how to actually cook is a skill they will need well into adulthood. Just as everyone needs to know how to pick up after themselves, everyone needs to eat.

Again, having children cook alongside of you for a while, as they learn how to cook certain things will be a great help. The right tools will also help make the task safer and easier. In the case of teaching my son to make pancakes and French toast, I found having an electric griddle to be the safest, most effective way to make those meals.

Other simple "starter" foods and cooking chores to start off include:

- Grilled Cheese Sandwiches
- Scrambled Eggs
- Raman Noodle Soup
- Baking Cookies
- Peeling veggies with a safe peeler
- Kneading bread dough

A Dozen Kitchen Safety Rules

The following twelve safety rules are good principles to keep in mind and to help your children learn while working in the kitchen.

Just as everyone needs to know how to pick up after themselves, everyone needs to eat.

1. Start cooking with a reasonably clean kitchen

For example, make sure there are no small spills on the floor, and your work area is cleared before you start to cook.

2. Before touching food, always wash your hands, and make sure nails are clean

Even when our hands look clean, they may not be. After handling eggs, meat or poultry, immediately wash your hands with soap to keep from spreading any potential germs. It also goes without saying to be careful when working in the kitchen when you are sick, and wash your hands frequently during flu season. This will help to keep sickness from spreading to the rest of the family via the kitchen.

3. If you have long hair, pull it back

Tying long hair back keeps hair from getting in your food, or falling near a hot surface or moving gadget.

I actually know someone with long tresses who got her hair caught in her standing mixer *Ouch!* Tie it back. No one wants to find hair in their food, and no one wants to find their hair in a mixer either!

An apron also keeps your clothing tighter against your body so it does not fall into the food you are working with, or any hot or wet surface. You should also roll up long sleeves when working in the kitchen.

4. Never put hot glass ware, plates, or ceramic servers on a cold surface or in cold water

When using hot ceramic or glass ware, do not ever take it from something hot and put it on or near something cold, until it has had a chance to cool slowly.

When using hot ceramic or glass ware, do not ever take it from something hot and put it on or near something cold, until it has had a chance to cool slowly.

5. Turn Your Handles In

Especially in a household of young children and pets, do not ever let your handles of pots and pans hang over the edge of the stove. This is not limited to households with young children, as anyone (including you!) can accidentally snag a pot handle that is hanging out. It is always best to turn them inward, toward the center of the stove. You should never leave any handle, especially of a sharp knife, hanging over the edge of a counter top, where a little person might grab it.

6. Be Careful of Steam Burns

When you are draining out something that was boiling in a hot liquid, such as when draining pasta, be very careful about steam burns. Sometimes the burns caused by steam can be just as bad as sticking your hand in a boiling pot of water.

7. Don't put sharp or fragile things into a sink full of soapy water

When you are filling up a big, sudsy sink full of hot water to soak dirty dishes, do not put anything sharp (like knives) or fragile (like glasses) into the hot water. Someone sticking their hands blindly into soapy water can easily be cut by sharp or broken objects in it.

8. Avoid Cross Contamination in your Cutting Boards, Towels, and Rags

Because of the potential bacteria from raw meats and eggs, it is important to use a separate cutting board for meats and poultry only. Soak this cutting board in bleach each time you use it, to kill any germs.

9. Keep flammables away from stove

I suppose it goes without saying that you want to keep flammable things away from the stove.

Do not let towels or any other cloth dangle near a flame of a gas stove or a heating element of an electric stove. Be careful of your hair, your clothing, your jewelry, and your hot pads when near the stove. Even the wooden handles of kitchen tools can catch fire, potentially, so use caution when working near the stove, and help your children to use caution around the stove.

Sometimes the burns caused by steam can be just as bad as sticking your hand in a boiling pot of water.

The kids are insisting I share my own little story of flammables and the stove. This is one of those lessons learned the hard way.

I was out of my normal cleaner for the stove top, but I did have a can of foaming bath cleaner. I figured that would probably clean up the stove top in a pinch. As I said in the section on all natural cleaners, I normally use white vinegar and the like. Following some unemployment, we were given some basics, including some cleaners and toiletries, which I was happy to have. But, I wasn't thinking when I set about to use them.

Did you know that foaming bathroom cleaner bursts into flames when used near a pilot light?

Me neither.

Thankfully, after the initial whoosh, the flames were gone. Lesson learned.

10. There should be no dangling or wet cords

Do not let the cords of electric appliances dangle off of work surfaces where a young child can grab them, and pull the appliance on top of themselves. This can be very dangerous when it contains hot foods. Of equal importance is not letting your cords or electrical appliances to get wet.

11. Use dry pot holders and trivets

When you are handling a hot pot, pan, or piece of bake ware, be sure that the pot holder you are using is dry. A wet pot holder is not going to protect you from the heat of the cookware, and you likely will not feel the heat until you are already carrying the pot or pan!

Do not let towels or any other cloth dangle near a flame of a gas stove or a heating element of an electric stove. Be careful of your hair, your clothing, your jewelry, and your hot pads when near the stove.

When placing hot cookware on the table, always use a trivet to set the pot down on, so as to not burn your table, or table cloth.

12. Never put food on any surface you would not eat from.

I think this is pretty self explanatory, don't you? If you won't eat off of it, don't prepare food on it.

15
Training Teenagers

During the period in my life when I had five children ages six and under, I would occasionally have some presumably well intentioned person walk up to me and point out that I'm going to have five teenagers at once, and I'd probably be sorry for it. I'm not sure why they felt they just had to share that happy news with me, but it happened more than once. I wasn't really sure what horrors may await me when I had teenagers, but I was trusting that my kids didn't have to turn completely psycho when they hit thirteen.

Teens are capable of a lot more than our society gives them credit for.

Guess what?

Children don't have to turn into the cultural norm for "teenagers" as soon as they are in the double digits. *Thank God.*

Teens are capable of a lot more than our society gives them credit for. In our family, we view these years as preparation for adulthood. We've tried to sit down and make a sort of "bucket list", but for entering adulthood. It's a list of things we want to remember to train our young people to do before we launch them into adulthood.

At this age, in our house, they are all pretty well-skilled in different household chores. Occasionally, some training and reminders still needs to be done.

As I lay recovering from my gall bladder surgery, I remember hearing a loud "boom", my husband making sure everyone was okay, and then the sound of my husband saying *"Your mom isn't going to be happy when she sees this."*

Oh, yeah. Nothing makes you feel better after a surgery quite like those words after a loud boom.

Curiosity finally got the best of me, and I crawled down the stairs to see what exploded. As it turns out, someone ignored my kitchen safety rule about not putting ice cold water into a fresh-from-the-oven glass pan.

Thankfully no one was hurt, and glass pans are easily found at the local Walmart. Let's just say, after hearing that really scary "boom", no one has put a hot glass pan on a cold surface again. Some lessons stick better with experience.

Exactly what kind of training and responsibilities are involved at this stage depends on your household and your teens. This is a great time to help them learn some more in depth real world skills they'll need as they branch off on their own someday.

This is a great time to help them learn some more in depth real world skills they'll need as they branch off on their own someday.

Just a few months ago, I had a problem with my washing machine. The water kept running in it, and didn't shut off when it reached a certain point. I am the sort of woman who has had to learn how to fix these things myself, having a husband who works all sorts of crazy hours. This made for a great time to show the teens how to figure out what is wrong and how to fix the situation. So, I took them, step by step, through troubleshooting the problem, Googling the problem, figuring out if there is a cheap fix to the problem (there was – under $1), and fixing the problem.

This doesn't mean that they are instant washing machine repair people, any more than I am. It does mean that they know how to figure out if a problem is something they can fix easily themselves though. They will, hopefully, be a little less intimidated to try to fix their own appliances some day.

Over the last few years, we've tried to help them learn more about some of these common household repairs. We live in an older house, with things constantly breaking, and no money to hire repair people for things we could handle ourselves. This has resulted in me getting used to doing quite a bit myself.

While teaching the kids how to properly care for and clean up in the bathroom, I've also taken the time, when the occasion arises, to show them how to fix basic things like repairing the chain inside the toilet that makes the handle work, which seems to come loose every few months.

The kids have also worked with me in patching lath and plaster walls, replacing kitchen faucets, fixing clogs without nasty chemicals, and other simple, common repairs that strike each of us every now and then.

Other household tasks I have tried to teach my teens include:

- Caring for special clothing
- Stain removal
- Managing a meal
- Supervising (but not bossing around) younger siblings
- Checking the fluids in the automobiles
- Checking tire pressure in the car
- Hanging a picture frame
- Sinking wall anchors for hanging things up
- Fixing and hanging curtain rods
- Frugal grocery shopping and meal planning
- Baby-sitting skills

I've also taken time to teach my kids how to do some basic clothing repair. For example, we've practiced how to sew on a button, or how to fix a rip when it's in a seam. We've learned how to cover a worn out knee in work pants. Sewing simple items from a pattern or from scratch is also handy to know. My one daughter made several throw pillows from scrap fabrics I had, without a pattern.

Each of my teens seems to have their own specialties, and areas of expertise by this age. As I said, my son loves to cook, especially breakfast foods. I let them work within their favorite tasks.

Part Three:
Final Thoughts
on the Path

16
Tone of Voice

About six years ago, a friend came to stay during the week around my birthday, which was a nice surprise. She had two very young children at the time, a preschooler and an infant. Because I know life works better with some routines in place, we tried to keep our routine as much as possible, while still having fun and enjoying our guests. So, we relaxed up on some chores to make time for people.

One day, my friend was commenting on how organized I was and how nicely our household seemed to flow.

"You say it quietly and calmly, and your kids do it. How did you get them to do that?"

After I wiped away the tears of laughter (I had never been called organized in the area of household management before), I asked her what exactly she meant.

"This house just seems to flow well, and you guys work together well. It's also your tone of voice. You say it quietly and calmly, and your kids do it. How did you get them to do that?"

I had to stop and think a bit.

Just as I'd not classify me as organized in domestic matters, I'd also not classify myself or my family as quiet or calm. We're pretty loud folk. We love to laugh. We're a little obnoxious and snarky. As a child I was quiet and shy. That most definitely doesn't describe me any more.

When I think of quiet and calm, I think of people like Michelle Duggar, mom on the *19 Kids and Counting* TV program, who always has this sweetly angelic disposition that I clearly do not have. I admire her, but I also know that just as my mom and I were wired different, Michelle and I are also wired differently. And that's okay. We're individuals.

As my friend and I talked about it, I realized part of my apparent "quietness" was not so much my disposition as much as a choice to make sure my children obey me without me raising my voice or having to yell.

Childhood Memories

Thinking back to my childhood, and even your childhood, I think we all can remember that mom may have called for us, or asked us to do things, but we didn't obey straight away. We knew that we didn't have to actually leave our fun until her voice reached a certain decibel level. We all knew what tone of voice meant that mom finally means business.

One of my friends, who lived nearby, was a perfect example of this.

We knew that we didn't have to actually leave our fun until mom's voice reached a certain decibel level.

We'd be merrily playing in my backyard, and her mom would calmly ask for her to come home for dinner in five minutes.

Five minutes would come and go, and we'd still be playing. We knew the routine by now. It wasn't urgent that she get home just yet.

Her mom would come outside, and slightly more irritated, she'd ask her to come home for dinner, with the tone of her voice reflecting her rising irritation.

She wasn't irritated enough to listen to yet though. We knew we still had more time.

She'd do this a few more times, each time she'd get more irritated, a little louder, and a little more shrill.

Finally, the cue that play time was over! Mrs. Jones would scream at the top of her lungs in a very shrill voice, "Chris-TEEEEN-AHHHHHHHHHHHHH!"

Okay, now she means business. Now we obey. Chris would hop the fence, and scurry on home as quickly as possible.

Now, obviously, as an adult who sees the value in children obeying parents, I know we should have obeyed at the first request. But, we had been trained, however indirectly, that we didn't really need to obey until that final shrill call from the next street over.

Counting to Three

A lot of us parents, though we may not realize it, train our children not to listen to us until we get to that point of red-faced, shrill voiced, loud scream. How do we do this? It's simple.

We don't make them obey the first time we ask.

When my oldest was very young, I would count to three, and by three, she had to obey. Most of the time, by the time I got to three, I was a little more agitated about the situation. You could hear it in the tone of my voice.

An older woman at our church asked me, "If she can obey on three, why can't she obey on one?"

Many of us train our children not to listen to us until we get to that point of red-faced, shrill voiced, loud scream. How do we do this? It's simple. We don't make them obey the first time we ask.

I had to think about that one for a moment. Hmm. Why can't she obey on "one"?

After getting some counsel from some ladies who have successfully raised some great children, I set about to get my children obeying me when I asked.

This took some time, of course, but I tried (by God's grace) not to allow them to get into the habit where I had to be on the verge of an aneurysm before they listened. The scope of this book is such that, if I were to take the time to go into all of the nitty gritty of child training, which was explained in better detail in other books, I'd probably triple the size of this book.

Although I can't say that I agree 100% with everything in each of these books, I do find them to be quite useful in the principles of child-rearing:

- *The Strong Willed Child* by Dr. James Dobson (I figured I needed this for "Baby Macguyver")

- *Creative Correction* by Lisa Wechel
- *Making Children Mind without Losing Yours*, Dr. Kevin Lehman and Randy Carlson (The Parent Talk radio program was also a big help)
- *Shepherding a Child's Heart* by Tedd Tripp
- *The Five Love Languages* by Dr. Gary Chapman

I also, by the way, allow them to say something like, "Can I finish this up really quick, or do you need me right this instant?" I know that I don't shift from one thing to another easily either, so I grant them that, especially if they are really into something.

The point is, if you allow your children to ignore you when you ask nicely, and only enforce obedience by the time you are ready to blow, then don't be surprised if they wait until that point to obey you each time. You've allowed it to become a habit.

If you allow your children to ignore you when you ask nicely, and only enforce obedience by the time you are ready to blow, then don't be surprised if they wait until that point to obey you each time.

The Screaming Momma

Most of us don't want to become the screaming momma. We don't ever plan to be that woman. No child ever wants their mom to be that woman. Sometimes it happens though.

I think any one of us moms who have been in the store and listened to some woman verbally berate and cajole her kids into minding her while they ignore her until her voice got loud and nasty enough have thought, "Those poor kids!" We usually don't have a whole lot of respect for mom. The kids apparently don't respect her either.

None of us sets out to be that mom, but at one point or another, sometimes we wind up being that mom...the mom who completely loses her cool and cuts loose verbally at the kids who realize that maybe now is a good time to do what she asked.

I want to encourage you. We don't have to be that way.

If we make our kids listen to us before our voices are loud and we're screaming away, we don't have to get to that point.

None of us likes it.

Moms don't want to be screaming mommas, right? Kids don't want to be screamed at, either. Though it may take some time (depending on the ages of your kids) to get them to listen straight away, before you raise your voice, or to get them out of the habit of only listening when you are ready to blow your lid, having children who listen to you when you ask calmly and quietly is priceless. It truly does make for a peaceful home.

It's Okay to Say You're Sorry

Talking with my children and husband, as I worked through the final edits of this book, one of the things each of my kids mentioned was that they remember that I always said I was sorry when I got upset, or yelled, or otherwise was not a joyful momma towards them.

I know that, as adults, we sometimes feel like we need to at least look like we have it all together. The truth is, we probably don't.

When you, as a parent, make a mistake, it's okay to say you're sorry. In all likelihood, your kids won't respect you less. They may actually respect you more.

> *As adults, we sometimes feel like we need to at least look like we have it all together. It's okay to say you're sorry when you make mistakes.*

17

Allowances and Wages

I think most parents wrestle with the question of whether or not to pay their children for the chores they do around the house. On the "pro" side, allowances can encourage a child to keep pressing on. Let's face it. Would you or your spouse go to work if you weren't getting paid? Probably not. On the "con" side, the argument could be made that no one pays us to make our beds, so why pay them for things that are their responsibility anyway.

Larger jobs do usually come with a certain wage attached, allowing them to earn money for youth activities and camp.

In our own family, we've wrestled with exactly how to handle this. Our method, which works for us, is to not pay for everyday type chores (picking up after oneself, doing the dishes, and general clean up). When our children were little, they earned a small amount (ten cents per job), but now that they are older, we have changed how we handled this.

When my children were still quite young, but were starting to be more autonomous, we made a rule where, if you did the job you got paid, and if you forgot to do the job and I had to do it for you, I got paid out of *your* money. Obviously, I didn't need the dime. But, this kept them on their toes as we started to encourage our children to work more independently.

Now, larger jobs do usually come with a certain wage attached, allowing them to earn money for youth activities and camp.

Some of those larger jobs include:

- Mowing the lawn

- Washing the car
- Washing the dogs
- Weeding the garden
- Washing the walls
- Babysitting
- Cleaning the basement
- Shoveling snow
- Cleaning and defrosting the downstairs freezer
- Sanding and painting the porches (which, in our house, needs to be done every other year)

Basically anything that is time consuming and not a regular job usually is a paying job. Whatever you decide regarding chores and allowances, the key is to be fair and be consistent in how you pay for these jobs, or any chores.

18
Praising Your Children

When we're in the thick of child-rearing, moms tend to be more tuned into correcting wrong behavior than praising right behavior. Instead of catching our children doing wrong, we need to work harder at catching them doing right.

I quoted this verse earlier, but I'd like to share this passage with you again,

"Fathers, provoke not your children to anger, lest they be discouraged."
(Colossians 3:21)

In raising our kids, we don't want to "provoke our children to wrath" and we don't want to discourage or dishearten them.

One important tool in our proverbial child-training toolbox is genuine gratitude for our kids and who they are, and expressing that thankfulness to them.

Thanks for Noticing

As a new mom, I found it a bit frustrating to spend all day long occupying a very active toddler, and repeatedly cleaning up the messes that were made, only to have no one notice what I did. If my husband came home during one of those moments right after she made a mess for the umpteenth time, it looked as though I hadn't done a thing all day.

That's pretty discouraging.

For stay at home moms, one of the most difficult things it seems we deal with is that lack of praise or positive feedback on what we did all day long. Most of the women I've talked to, who have had good jobs before motherhood have found that to be one of their biggest challenges.

Doesn't positive feedback on a job you worked hard on feel good?

Think about the last time you got some positive feedback or praise from someone on something you did. Did it make you feel like doing it again? How about working hard on something but having no one notice? Did you feel energized to do that again?

For most of us, having our work noticed makes us feel more encouraged the next time we do it, but feeling like we're being taken for granted seems to have the opposite effect.

So, what makes us think our kids are any different?

Oh, ouch.

Genuine praise for a job well done, and letting them know you appreciate them goes a long way in encouraging your children to keep pressing on in their helpfulness to you.

Doesn't positive feedback on a job you worked hard on feel good?

Just One Thing

If it is not your nature to be thankful, or to point out the good in others, decide to make it your new habit, over the next 21 days, to find just one thing to praise your children (and your mate) about. You'll be surprised and what kind of effect it has on others.

We all love to be told of a job well done, don't we? Be sure to let your children know you're thankful for a job well done.

Why stop at one thing, though? Once you're in the habit of expressing your thanks to your children, you don't just have to thank and praise them for one thing. Find as much as you can to genuinely thank them for. Encourage them in what they are doing right, and you'll find them doing it more and more.

19
Making Comparisons

When you have more than two children in your family, some things become more apparent to you, like the fact that every child is an individual. I mentioned earlier that I used to think of children as little empty vessels for us as parents and educators to fill up, or blank slates that we write on.

Find just one thing to praise your children (and your mate) about. You'll be surprised and what kind of effect it has on others.

That's not at all correct.

Every child has gifts, talents, and natural abilities built in. They have unique personality traits, and they seem to handle different situations in unique ways.

One child handles constructive correction well, and another bursts into tears. One child understands instructions the first time, and another needs you to remind them ten times when first learning a new skill.

It's easier to thank and praise certain kids, because they do all things well. It's harder with their siblings who don't seem to "get it" the first time, or even the fifth time.

The child who is born with a strong organizational ability is a little easier to appreciate when it comes to keeping a room tidy, than her sister who creates piles everywhere in a sort of organized chaos.

One of the most destructive things we can do is to make our kids live in the shadow of their siblings, or forever trying to compete with their brother or sister who does things "better".

As we train our children, we need to appreciate and thank each child for their own unique skills, instead of comparing them to others.

Speaking in a Way They Understand

Earlier I mentioned that even those of us who were not born with the neatnik gene have to learn how to care for a home, and clean up after ourselves.

The kids who have a more natural ability in this area can be easier to train. Their brain sees messes and desires to clean those up in ways that we Slobalinas can't, at least not without training.

I have home schooled all of my children for all of their K-12 school years thus far. This means that, among other things, I have taught my kids how to read.

The first child learned to read quite easily. I found myself patting myself on the back. I was clearly good at this home schooling mom thing.

One of the most destructive things we can do is to make our kids live in the shadow of their siblings, or forever trying to compete with their brother or sister who does things "better".

The wind was let out of my sails when I attempted to teach one of my other kids how to read. They way his brain worked was at odds with the curriculum we were using. It worked fine for all of the other kids, but with him, I needed to switch gears and find something that worked for him, to get him reading, in spite of his dyslexia.

The hard part, for me, was the fact that I found the new curriculum to be idiotically boring and repetitive to an extreme. I couldn't see how this could possibly work, because it isn't the way I learn. But, it worked for him.

On the flip side, he was and is really wired to understand math, computer programming, and all manner of technical things in ways that astound me. Now 17 years old, he is one of the go-to tech guys at our church, and works hard in the sound booth and audio/visual department. Last month, I found him hovered over a laptop first thing in the morning.

"Where did that laptop come from, honey?" I asked. It didn't look at all familiar.

"Oh, Mrs. So and So broke the screen on it, and she was upset that she hadn't backed it up, so I'm going to hook it up to this here, and (insert techno-babble that I didn't understand even though I have a degree in computer graphics and thought I taught him everything he knows)...so I nearly have her back up DVD done."

Among my other kids, one perpetually gave me the doe-in-the-headlights look whenever we worked on math, until I switched methods with her. Another child inexplicably taught herself Mandarin Chinese, and was recently conversing with the waitress at the Chinese take out, though I had to teach her to read English using a lot of whole-word methodology instead of predominately phonics. Now I see that her difficulty with phonics may have helped her with the Chinese. Life is strange.

What's the point I'm trying to make?

Not everyone learns the same thing in the same way.

Not everyone learns the same thing in the same way.

As you train your kids, if something that worked with child one isn't working for child two, maybe they need you to switch the method you're using. Try different ideas for teaching skills if, after some time, a child still can't "see" it. When I was a child, I couldn't see (try as I might) the mess in my room that bugged my mom. I can see it now, though. It just took time and learning in a way that made sense to me in how I am wired.

20
Encouraging Initiative

Having worked lots of odd jobs over the years before having children, I got to see first hand the blessings of someone who takes initiative while on the job (whether at home or for pay), and the frustration of being a manager of those who only do the bare minimum. From what I could tell during both of my jobs as assistant manager, it seems to me that the ability to look around and see what needs to be done without being told is a skill that very few people enter adulthood with.

I didn't really learn this skill until I was left in charge of a restaurant one day when my boss had an emergency. I didn't want to disappoint him, as I wanted the kitchen to look as good as when he had to run out of there to the hospital. During that very long afternoon under the burden of leadership as a sophomore in college, I suddenly realized how annoying it is to have people look at you and ask "I washed this pan over here. What should I do now?" when it should have been obvious. It took all of my composure to look at them and say, calmly, "Why don't you wash the other pans from the same pile?"

I had instant sympathy for my boss and my mother. Being in charge is not always as glamorous as we imagine it being. It is frustrating when you have adults who can't see that, if one dirty pan needs to be washed then perhaps all of them do.

One of the reasons why I like to give my children step by step instructions for how to clean certain things is because this helps them to have clear direction for cleaning up an area. The "next level" in teaching them step by step how to clean something is to help them notice when it needs to be cleaned, without mom or dad asking them to do it.

Pick it Up

This starts, as with chores, with picking up after yourself. If you drop something, spill something, or otherwise make a mess, you stop what you're doing and you clean it up. This sort of training can be really inconvenient for us as moms, because that means *we* have to stop what *we're* doing, and direct our children back to the mess, and have them pick it up, when it would be far easier to tear of a paper towel and wipe up the spill ourselves.

While visiting someone's home, I watched this in action. Their twenty year old son, who still lives at home and can't hold a job, poured himself a glass of milk. He left the fridge door open, left the cap to the milk on one counter, the milk on the table, and a spill. Mom stopped her conversation with me, got up, wiped the milk, put the cap back on, and returned the milk to the fridge. If he were two, I could understand this, but at twenty I found it sad.

The ability to look around and see what needs to be done without being told is a skill that very few people enter adulthood with.

Later, on our way out, we noticed he left the half drunk glass of milk on the rail to the porch on a 90 degree day, which she also cleaned up promptly. Mom didn't do him any favors by cleaning up after him. My husband and I wondered on our way home if her molly-coddling of her son is part of the reason why he can't seem to hold a job. As a former assignment manager, *I sure wouldn't want someone like him working for me.*

Last week, one of my daughters was giving out free hair cuts (she is actually quite good at cutting hair, and is thinking about cosmetology school). The problem is, she left hair all over a rug, and then left for an appointment she had, leaving the mess behind.

With her not home, I nearly cleaned it up for her. After all, she cleaned up most of it, but left it on the little area rug. The problem is, she's done this a couple of times now when cutting hair, so I needed to nip this in the bud. The rug waited for her to get home.

Getting them to clean up after their own messes is not just about the mess itself.

No, it's about teaching our children the valuable life skills of personal responsibility and initiative. These are skills that help our children succeed in whatever they are called to do.

21
Consequences

We all need a little accountability in our lives.

What do I mean by accountability? When you ask your children to do something, make sure they really do. And, if they don't, make sure there is a consequence to that choice they've made.

When you are first training your children, you'll be working alongside them until they are older, at least most of the time. There's some built in accountability right there. Mom is constantly standing there, reminding them, encouraging them, and helping them along the way.

There comes a point though, when we are encouraging personal initiative and responsibility, where we have to let them try (and possibly fail) without mom standing over them with reminders. As my children grew, I made sure that my reminders were less and less frequent, and that there were logical consequences to not doing what was asked of them.

I had a great example of this just last month.

As I wrote in the chapter on decluttering, we recently did some small fix-ups in one of the girls' rooms. Our daughters helped paint and I asked one of my girls to please wash the paint rollers and brushes. I had to go to an appointment, so I told her I'd like for her to take care of it while I was away.

When I got back, and it was time for us to do another layer of paint, I was disappointed but not entirely surprised to find that she had not washed all of the rollers. She came upstairs to help me paint, which she was really enjoying, and I told her we couldn't get started until all of the paint was off the rollers.

Now, I am no fool. I know that dried latex paint is not coming off of a roller, and it is certainly cheaper to just buy a new roller. In fact, she didn't know it, but I had a whole case of them in the basement, as I bought them at a warehouse store.

The point of this exercise was to show her why timeliness was essential in cleaning the paint off the rollers. You don't put that job off until later. Knowing my children as I do, I knew this particular teen has some issues with forgetting what she was supposed to be doing and moving on to something more enjoyable within a few minutes unless I am there to prod her along. I wanted to help her not need that constant prodding, by showing her the consequence of not doing what she was told, when she was told.

The other kids were all a bit sympathetic. I think each of them have spent some quality time trying to clean dry latex paint off of a cheap roller for the same reasons. This is a great object lesson in why we complete jobs in a timely fashion.

I wanted to help her not need that constant prodding, by showing her the consequence of not doing what she was told, when she was told.

I set a timer for a half an hour. When the timer went off, I went upstairs.

"How's it going? Are you making progress?" I asked. I already knew that answer, of course.

"Nooooooo! This won't come off. It's all dried on there! I tried everything. Maybe if I soak it a little...."

"Do you know what I think would clean paint off a roller?" I asked.

"What?" she asked eagerly.

"If you were to do it when it was still wet, instead of waiting for it to dry on there."

"Uh....right. I'm sorry mom. I was going to do it, and then I had an idea for a drawing and...."

"I know. I saw your sketchbook on the table and I figured that's what happened...."

"What are we going to do?" she asked.

"First, the next time I tell you something needs to be done right now, please remember this little object lesson. Next, go down to the basement. On the work bench, there's a whole case of those."

She and I both laughed a bit, and did our next layer of paint. When we were done, there was a new test.

"Honey, will you wash off these rollers?"

"Yes momma!"

I can assure you, those ones were cleaned well before the paint even started to dry.

Now, this is not something you do with a young child. A younger child cannot reason or think things through logically in the same way an older or teen can. This only works with an older child who can logically learn the lesson you're trying to teach.

Why Logical Consequences?

In the "real world", there are consequences for our actions. If you do "this"...then "that" will happen.

So, why I am talking about using logical consequences? Why not just ground them from the computer or make them write "I will obey my momma" 100 times?

In the "real world", there are consequences for our actions. If you do "this"...then "that" will happen.

In the real world, if I were to go off and do something more fun, and leave my paint rollers to clean up later, I'd probably spend a half an hour trying to clean them before realizing how dumb it was for leaving them be until they were dry, and I'd have to buy new ones. In fact, I did that the first time I painted in our first home. I only did that mistake once.

When your kids do something like this, try to think of what would happen if they did this as adults for the first time, and allow them to reap the consequence for a short time. After all, the goal of training our children and disciplining them for mistakes is not punitive, that is, to punish them. The supreme goal should be to teach our children right from wrong in a way that they will always remember, so as to avoid that mistake again.

Obviously, I wasn't about to let my poor daughter scrub at

those rollers all night. But I let it last just long enough for her to realize that paint needs to be cleaned up when wet, because it's not coming off of a cloth roller when dry no matter what you do to it.

22
Setting an Example

I have, in the past, had the bad habit of walking away from messes I made myself. I would step over a piece of paper on the floor, or leave dribbled coffee on the counter until the next scheduled kitchen cleaning time. I didn't even really realize this until I had children who did the same, leaving it for *me* to clean up.

Let me tell you, realizing I was setting a poor example in this area certainly helped me to overcome my rather bad habit like few other things could have.

As a mom you may have had the experience of looking at your child and seeing some of your bad habits staring back at you through their angelic little face. It's humbling, isn't it?

As with most things in effective motherhood, training children with a good work ethic starts with setting a good example.

As I touched on earlier, children will pick up on our attitudes rather quickly. When we have a poor attitude regarding work, our children are likely to take on that same attitude regarding work.

If we treat housework as something to dread, so will they.

If you are showing them that cleaning and work is something to begrudgingly tolerate until it's time to have fun, then don't expect your children to be cheerful about helping. You are not just training them to work, but you are also training an attitude about work. This is hard if we were trained with a not so great attitude about work.

I always viewed working around the house as a form of cruel and unusual punishment. You can imagine what a difficulty I had when I found myself "employed" as a stay at home mother with a young child. That attitude sucked the life out of my everyday life, since my everyday life consisted of those tasks I always associated with a very negative attitude. I knew that if I were to embrace my new career as at-home mommy to this precious little one, and give her a good example, I needed to check that attitude and change it.

I have found child training and raising (and even marriage for that matter) to be like sandpaper rubbing off my rough edges and those parts of me that needed to change. The Bible says that as iron sharpens iron, we sharpen each other (paraphrase of Proverbs 27:17). Specifically, Proverbs refers to our friends in this verse, but I think it is even more true within the context of our homes and families who see the good, bad and ugly on a daily basis.

Dealing with negative attitudes in my children that they clearly learned from me really is like sandpaper, smoothing off those rough bits in my personality. Our family gets to grow together in this and other areas.

23
Attitude Adjustments

As I train my children to be helpers, I am more concerned with their attitudes while they are doing the work, than their job performance itself. Obviously, I want them to do a good job, but if they are grumbling the whole time, I don't consider that to be very helpful.

I want my children to have a good work ethic, and a good attitude about the work they have to do. Work is a part of life, and so my thought is that they ought to have the right attitude when working.

Training children with a good work ethic starts with setting a good example.

Thoughts on Attitudes

Here are some additional thoughts on helping our children have a right attitude:

Know what is expected

If you don't know what the goal is, how are you going to know if you and the kids are hitting it or missing it? In regards to both chores and attitudes, be sure to have clear expectations. Based on what you see as an issue in your own home, come up with some goals and smaller benchmarks to work towards.

Next, don't just keep this to yourself. Discuss your current goal with your children before you have problems. Let them know what you want to work on with their attitude and yours. Very clearly let them know what the rewards and consequences are going to be too.

Have Clear Expectations for Work

Have clear expectations for the chores you're assigning too. Don't change what you expect from your kids. You're kids will be able to follow the rules better if they know what they are.

Be Thankful for their Helpfulness

Again, don't forget to thank them for being helpful. Let them know how much you appreciate their hard work and their willingness to help you out and to try.

Give Added Work

If an older child starts to cop an attitude about something, I usually will ask them if they'd like extra work. If the attitude doesn't improve, I will give it to them. I've found this to work quite well.

Have meaningful rewards for helpfulness with a good attitude

Give Out Meaningful Rewards

Having meaningful rewards for helpfulness with a good attitude can be of help too. I want to do all I can to encourage cheerful helpfulness. While I don't reward every little chore done with a good attitude, sometimes I will surprise my kids with a special treat after a period of time with great attitudes and helpfulness. For example, after a time of hard work in the garden, we may go up to a nearby city with a nice zoo and a free splash park for the afternoon. I try to do things that they enjoy, which will show them how much I appreciate their cheerful helpfulness.

What's the Problem?

When dealing with bad attitudes, I try to ask myself the following questions, to make sure there isn't some other reason for the problem. Obviously I still deal with the attitude, but sometimes some changes need to be made for the short term to help my child with their chore.

Is the chore within their skill level?

If you're asking more of your child than she is capable of doing, then she may likely develop a sour attitude towards that job.

Remember when your baby took her first steps? Did she learn to walk at exactly day 368 of her life? Did she learn to walk at exactly the same age that her peers did? Not likely.

Just because someone's chore chart says that your child should be able to do such and such, doesn't mean they are capable of it. You know your child better than anyone else. If something seems to be exhasperating them beyond just a normal learning curve, back off for a short time, and let them mature a bit more. Otherwise, you're just going to frustrate the both of you.

Are they "getting" what you're teaching and how you're teaching it?

A child who doesn't understand something usually gets frustrated, and translates that frustration into acting out or copping a bad attitude.

Just because someone's chore chart says that your child should be able to do such and such, doesn't mean they are capable of it.

I've shared some ways in which I've helped my children learn to do certain chores. None of these are the "One Right Way" to do things. They are just suggestions to get your creative juices flowing.

If a child is frustrated, they may not be understanding how you are teaching. Try to break the steps down more. Give them more manageable "bites", instead of the whole chore at once. For example, folding a towel, instead of learning to fold all laundry. Try to find other ways to teach the skill you're trying to convey, so that they understand better.

If a child seems particularly scattered, breaking down a job into manageable steps, and frequent reminders are very helpful. A child who has some attention problems (diagnosed or not) usually will do better with you pointing out every little part of the chore. When teaching them to clean their room, for example, they will likely need very detailed step by step instructions, over and over again until they finally get it.

How's your attitude been?

Finally, check your own attitude. Her attitude may very well be a mirror reflecting your own.

24
Rescuing Cinderella

As you can probably tell from what I've written thus far, I'm all for teaching responsibility. I want my children to develop a good work ethic as they are growing up.

On the other hand, I don't want my older kids to feel like they are here to lighten my load. They are still kids after all. I am using household chores to train them towards a good work ethic and to prepare them for the day when they'll be living on their own. But, I don't want my kids feeling like Cinderella, always working and never able to go to the Ball.

> *I don't want my kids feeling like Cinderella, always working and never able to go to the Ball.*

One of the ways a mom can keep their older kids from feeling too overworked is to give the chore in question to the youngest child able to do it. This way, the older kids are not too overwhelmed with the bulk of the chores.

Now that all of my children are able to do each chore, we have them more evenly distributed, where everyone has a day to do specific jobs. That's where the chore chart does come in – we look at it to see who's day it is to do dishes, and who sweeps the living room.

I allowed some autonomy in the creation of this new chore chart, now that we have a house full of capable teens. They actually hashed it out together this time around, with very little input from me.

When one sibling has an activity on a day when they have certain chores, sometimes they can switch with their siblings or barter with them in some other way to have the night off. My girls tend to be in high demand as of late as babysitters, and my son is frequently running the sound booth for activities or doing other technical things with the audio/visual aspects of our church. I allow them to be free to delegate to siblings, but not to take advantage of it.

Chores and housework are a part of life, and this has become just another aspect of helping them learn to balance what needs to be done with other responsibilities and commitments they might have.

Epilogue: Thank You

T*hank you for reading.*
If you can do me one favor, please go to Amazon.com and rate this book, give it a review. This will help more people find this book. If you didn't like it, let me know how I can improve upon it in any future editions. You can also check this book's website and blog, www.BeyondtheChoreChart.com, for updates, Q and A's, and more.

If there's something you feel I didn't explain clearly enough in this book, please drop me a line in the contact form on this site, so I can edit future editions of this book.

You may also want to check out other books I have available for Amazon Kindle or as print books. There should be a link on my main web site, www.JoyfulMomma.com. As of this writing, these include

Joyful Momma's Guide to Shopping and Cooking Frugally

Joyful Momma's Guide to Quiet Times in Loud Households

Both of these books, as well as the one you're reading now, have been printed in Paperback as well and are also available on Amazon.com or on my website.

Thank you again,

Kimberly

Step 1 - pick up toys after playing

Step 2 - make bed every day

Step 3 - dirty clothes in hamper/chute
      & put away clean clothes
      (put signs on dressers)

Step 4 - Set the table & clearing table

Step 5 - Unload dishwasher/load dishwasher

Step 6 - Cook w/ mom

Step 7 - sweeping floor

Step 8 - clean bedroom

Step 9 - Teach Annie to do laundry
      (do it w/ her for a year)

Step 10 - Bathroom - keep towels off floor
      wipe down sink, toilet & bath tub
      & spills on floor

Step 11 - sweeping/vaccuming (wait til everything
    from top to bottom is clean.

come up w/ goals & clear expectations &
    share w/ kids.
      - picking up & cleaning after
        yourself
      - everything has a place - put it
        back
      - have good attitudes when
        cleaning.

Made in the USA
Lexington, KY
29 May 2015